MAKING RIGHTS REAL

FOR FUTURE GENERATIONS

MAKING RIGHTS REAL FOR FUTURE GENERATIONS
A CEDAW WORKBOOK

Readers are encouraged to go to www.MissionPointPress.com to contact the author, or to contact the publisher about how to buy this book in bulk at a discounted rate.

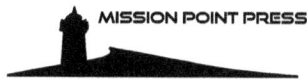
MISSION POINT PRESS

Published by Mission Point Press
2554 Chandler Rd.
Traverse City, MI 49696
(231) 421-9513
www.MissionPointPress.com

ISBN: 978-1-961302-37-2
Library of Congress Control Number:

Printed in the United States of America

MAKING RIGHTS REAL

FOR FUTURE GENERATIONS

A CEDAW WORKBOOK

Krishanti Dharmaraj
and Soon-Young Yoon

MISSION POINT PRESS

FORWARD

Making Rights Real for Future Generations is a workbook on the local implementation of human rights. The booklet was written by Krishanti Dharmaraj and Soon-Young Yoon and published by the Cities for CEDAW History and Futures Project. This workbook refers to a publication by WILD (2006) that focused on implementing CEDAW in US cities and is written to reflect the goals and objectives of the Cities for CEDAW campaign launched in 2014 by the NGO Committee on the Status of Women, New York. The writers wish to acknowledge and thank everyone who has contributed to making this publication possible. Youmna Chalala, Patti Chang, Robin Levi, and Cosette Thompson made valuable contributions during the adoption of an ordinance and implementation in San Francisco. Members of the NGOCSW/New York at the start of the Cities for CEDAW campaign included Houry Geudelekian, Ivy Koek, Bette Levy, Susan O'Malley, Angeline Martin, Padmini Murthy, Mary Ann Tarantula, and Kate Washburn. Jessica Pierson, co-director of the Cities for CEDAW History and Futures project with her team of dedicated researchers, have provided vital information about the campaign.

Krishanti Dharmaraj
Soon-Young Yoon

Table of Contents

What Is Cities For CEDAW?

In 1998, San Francisco became the first city in the world to adopt a human rights treaty, notably the Convention on the Elimination of all Forms of Discrimination against Women (CEDAW) as an ordinance. The architect of this historic event was Krishanti Dharmaraj, then Executive Director of Women's Institute for Leadership Development for Human Rights (WILD for Human Rights). She led a team in partnership with Patti Chang (President of the Women's Foundation of California) and Cosette Thomson (Director of Amnesty International, Western Region), some of whom attended the UN Fourth World Conference on Women held in Beijing in 1995. They were determined to bring women's human rights home but saw little chance for CEDAW ratification by the US government. At the same time, they wanted to respond to the negative impact on women of California's propositions 187 and 209 that violated the rights of immigrants and rolled back affirmative action.

A broad coalition included WILD for Human Rights in partnership with Amnesty International, the Women's Foundation, La Casa de las Madres, and the San Francisco Commission on the Status of Women and Human Rights Commission that endeavored to work closely with city officials such as President of the Board of Supervisors Barbara Kaufman, the mayor's office, and Head of Public Works Ed Lee. The two-year strategy that started in 1996 included public hearings on CEDAW articles, briefings to city departments and commissions, advocacy with the media, education and awareness programs for NGOs, the private sector, and students and youth leaders.

Implementation and accountability were ensured through a CEDAW implementation task force that included government officials, union representatives, and community-based organizations. Also, as a result of the ordinance, the city allocated $200,000 for a rights-based gender analysis of all city departments. Soon after, Berkeley, CA and Hawaii followed suit with their own CEDAW ordinances.

The Cities for CEDAW campaign began in 2014 as part of the celebration of the 20th anniversary of the UN Fourth World Conference on Women. Soon-Young Yoon, who was then Chair of the NGO Committee on the Status of Women/New York (NGOCSW/NY), saw the potential in a Cities for CEDAW campaign to commemorate Beijing plus 20.[1] The NGOCSW/NY executive committee thus requested Mayor Edwin Lee to be the peer leader for the United States mayors to pass a resolution in support of CEDAW at the US Conference of Mayors held in San Francisco that year. More than 200 mayors signed on to a CEDAW resolution which set the stage for a national campaign. The San Francisco Department on the Status of Women worked hand in hand with the Women's Intercultural Network (WIN) to join the Cities for CEDAW campaign. Following the launch of the campaign during the NGO Forum in 2014, there was a dramatic spike in local actions by international NGOs in collaboration with activists and governments.

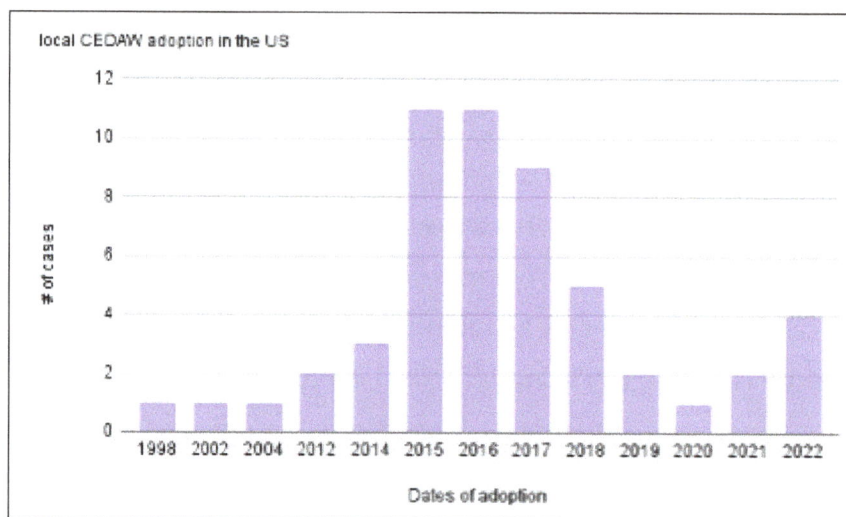

local CEDAW adoption in the US

(Source: Sarah Kimiko Ernst, "Network Dynamics of Grassroot Activism: The Case of "cities for CEDAW" in the United States," B.SC. Thesis, University of Twente, 2022)

Due to the efforts of feminist and women leaders in cities across the US, more than 70 jurisdictions—cities, counties, and states—have adopted CEDAW as an ordinance or resolution. This includes Los Angeles, CA, Salt Lake City, UT, Toledo, OH, Louisville, KY, and Cincinnati, OH, as well as Santa Clara and Miami-Dade counties, and all counties in the state of Hawaii. Statewide support came from California and Hawaii which strengthened local momentum in support of women's human rights. Priorities differed from one place to another and included a wide range of issues from sexual and reproductive health and rights, economic justice, racial and ethnic discrimination, trafficking, and equal pay in the private as well as public sectors. The adoption of CEDAW also fostered a culture of gender justice in city departments, introduced

---

1   Members of the NGOCSW/NY at the start of the Cities for CEDAW campaign included Houry Geudelekian, Ivy Koek, Bette Levy, Susan O'Malley, Angeline Martin, Padmini Murthy, and Mary Ann Tarantula.

(blue = ordinance and yellow = resolution)

gender-responsive budgeting, and nurtured innovation in the arts, public-private partnerships, housing, transport, and infrastructure planning, as well as delivery of education, health, and social services. Despite these advances, the US has yet to ratify CEDAW.[2]

---

2   In 1979, the United Nations General Assembly adopted CEDAW and as of August 2023, 189 member states have ratified this treaty. The United States remains the only industrialized country that has yet to ratify CEDAW. The US signed CEDAW in 1980, which formalized its intention to adopt the convention into national law, but the treaty is awaiting senate vote after two hearings in the US Senate Foreign Relations Committee. Numerous US cities, counties, and states have passed resolutions urging federal ratification.

Purpose of the Campaign

The short-term goal of the Cities for CEDAW campaign is to "make the global local" by promoting the adoption of CEDAW as an ordinance in cities, counties, and states to realize the human rights of girls and women of all ages. The long-term goal is to ensure that CEDAW is fully integrated—and implemented—with the 2030 sustainable development agenda at the local level to ensure inclusion, equity, and equality regardless of identity. The 2030 Agenda for Sustainable Development, adopted by all United Nations member states in 2015, "provides a shared blueprint for peace and prosperity for people and the planet, now and into the future. Goal 5 concerns Gender Quality."[3] The concept is simple: If we can weave women's human rights into the urban sustainable development agenda, we can change the course of cities not just for women, but for the whole world. It can also change the daily lives of women and girls. As Maimunah Mohd Sarif, Executive Director of Habitat has said, "If you can design a city for women, you have designed it for everyone."

> **Sustainable Development Goal Five (target 5.2)**
>
> *Eliminate all forms of violence against women and girls in the public and private spheres, including trafficking and sexual and other types of exploitation.*

Why is this important? First, more than 80 percent of Americans live in urban areas. By 2050, nearly 70 percent of the world's women and girls will live in cities.[4] The three major issues facing the world are inequalities, climate change, and violence/conflicts. These disproportionately affect women and girls. Women are unequally affected by the housing crisis, violations of labor standards, restrictions on sexual and reproductive health care, income inequalities, and unsafe public spaces. They have less influence in policy making, city leadership and decision-making.

Second, cities are becoming the epicenter of political, economic, cultural growth, and innovation. As the home of the world's greatest concentration of cities, the industrialized countries have a critical role to play in achieving the 2030 sustainable development goals, including those related to climate change and the environment. Equally important, cities can innovate and measure rapid change, even when the national government cannot—or will not—act. This includes addressing political, economic, cultural, and social inequality.

Some analysts suggest that the Cities for CEDAW campaign provides a much-needed landing

---

3   See https://sdgs.un.org/2030agenda

4   UN Conference of Parties, Outreach Issues, Warsaw, 2013, www.cop19.gov.pl.

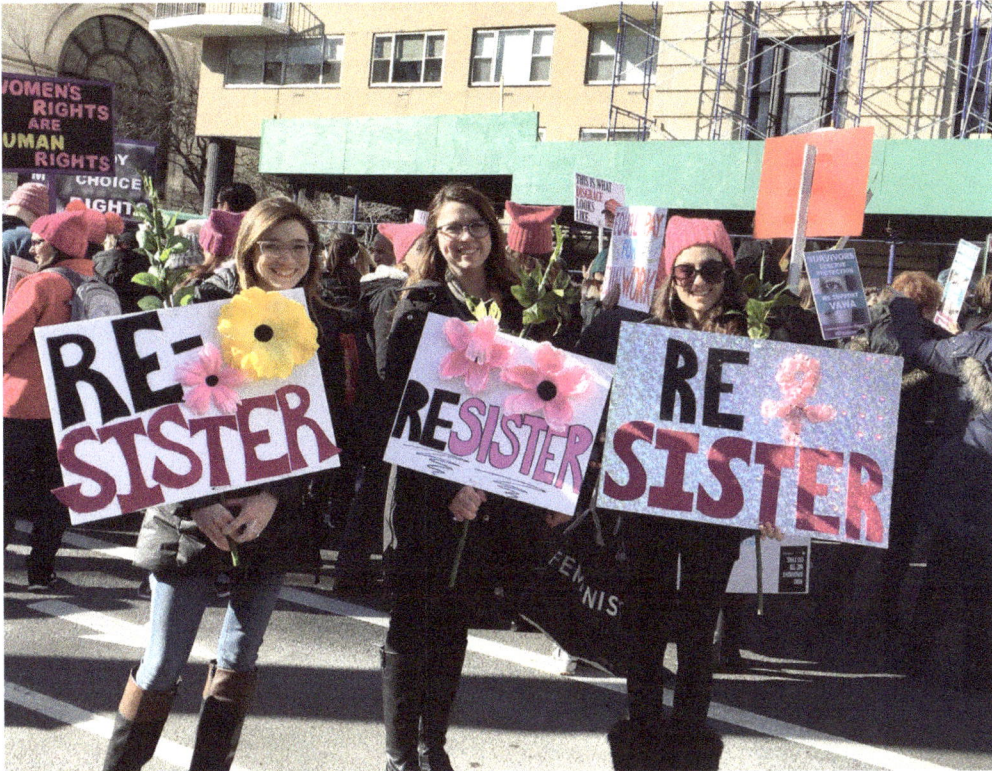

platform for the spontaneous energy unleashed by the women's marches and racial justice movements. These have been increasingly important as opposition to women's human rights have gained ground.[5] As some advocates have said, "For us, CEDAW is the roadmap on how to include gender and racial equality in city government." Marches mobilize, but CEDAW guides policies to get the work done.

The Purpose of This Handbook

The purpose of this handbook is to learn from the past decade of action, glean lessons learned, and propose methods and strategies to keep the Cities for CEDAW campaign innovative and strong. It is not intended to be a prescription for success, but rather, it is a platform for discussion, a blueprint of action to be adapted to each local condition.

The handbook provides a brief overview of CEDAW principles, tools of analysis of implementing CEDAW in cities, as well as monitoring and evaluation. Case studies are provided, drawing from the highly successful Cities for CEDAW campaign currently active in more than 80 jurisdictions.

---

5   Organized opposition to the Cities for CEDAW campaigns has been documented in public hearings in California and Virginia.

The handbook should be used by a team of experts on women's human rights, climate change and environment, and leaders in the Cities for CEDAW campaign. The methodology is interactive and participatory, including direct instruction, multiple discussion opportunities, and case studies.

As you begin using this book, there are some historical, conceptual, and practical questions about human rights and the CEDAW treaty that are useful to explore. The answers to these questions will provide the foundation for bringing human rights to your local community. We encourage you to keep returning to them.

The Relevance of Human Rights

FOR DISCUSSION

- How do you define dignity?
- How do you define well-being?
- What does equality and equity mean to you?
- What do people need in your community to express their full humanity?
- What will be necessary for individuals, organizations, businesses, and governments to fully recognize the dignity and equality of each person?

What Are Human Rights?

Human rights are the fundamental rights of each person to the conditions that allow us to express our full humanity. At this point in history, fulfilling all human rights is an ideal but not a reality. Improving the conditions of society to protect the dignity, well-being, and humanity of all people is a guiding principle of the human rights framework.

Human rights are:

- **Universal**
  Human rights belong to everyone in all their diversities. Across national borders, the same human rights standards apply equally to all people, and all governments are equally accountable for upholding these standards. This includes unhoused/homeless, displaced, undocumented, incarcerated, and transgender people, those living under occupation, and those stigmatized by society due to their status.

- **Interdependent**

  Human rights are connected; it is necessary to uphold all rights of all people in order to protect any rights. If one group's rights are violated, all individuals become vulnerable. Also, a person's ability to exercise human rights depends on the simultaneous enforcement of civil, political, economic, social, and cultural rights. (For example, in order for women to lead lives free from violence, women's economic rights and right to health must be protected.) Most of the rights recognized in the US Bill of Rights are civil and political rights, and the US government historically has given precedence to these rights over economic, social, and cultural rights.

  > **Universal Declaration on Human Rights**
  >
  > *All human beings are born free and equal in dignity and rights. They are endowed with reason and conscience and should act towards one another in a spirit of amity.*

- **Indivisible**

  Human rights are inherent to each person and cannot be taken away.

What Is a Human Rights Framework?

A human rights framework is a set of ideas, values, and principles that promote the dignity of all people and lead toward constructing humane conditions in society. These values are developed through United Nations documents such as the Universal Declaration of Human Rights (UDHR), and other treaties. They include civil, political, economic, social, and cultural rights. Governments are obligated to respect (cannot directly violate rights), protect (ensure that a third party does not violate rights), and fulfill (will use all available resources to advance rights). Human rights advocates use these values to develop strategies for change.

How Are Human Rights Used at the Local Level?

Integrating human rights standards into your local work provides:

- **A Common Framework for Social and Political Change**

  The human rights framework offers a shared vision and principles.

- **A Proactive Value System**

  Rather than responding to threats or reacting to problems, working for human rights is about creating a world where each person's humanity is respected and protected.

- **Mechanisms for Accountability**

  Treaties are legally binding, and governments, corporations, and individuals can publicly be called upon to live up to their obligations.

- **The Ability to Work on Multiple and Interconnected Issues**

  Because it recognizes that all rights are interdependent, the human rights framework makes connections among social justice issues and strengthens multi-issue organizing.

- **Minimum Standards for Human Dignity**

  Human rights treaties describe and guarantee the conditions that people require to meet their basic needs. Subsequent work by the human rights organizations and movements have been dedicated to explaining and applying these guarantees.

- **A Comprehensive Framework that Allows for Diversity, Inclusion, and Equity of Communities**

  The human rights framework demands consideration of how people's identities and experiences intersect, and how this intersection affects their ability to enjoy their human rights.

- **A Connection to the Larger, Global Human Rights Movements**

  Although the human rights framework is new to many people in the United States, it is not new in the rest of the world. Community groups around the world are already using human rights language and tools to further their work. We can learn valuable strategies from them, and through collaboration we can address global issues.

QUESTIONS

- What are other benefits to using a human rights framework?
- What are some ways that local groups can integrate human rights standards in their work?
- What are some limitations to using human rights documents or the human rights framework?

How Can We Use Human Rights Standards?

1. **EDUCATION to Change Attitudes and Behaviors**
   Popular education about human rights will give people tools to understand and describe the issues of importance in their communities.

2. **ORGANIZING to Bring Principles of Social Justice into Your Communities**
   Community mobilization to uphold human rights can unify groups that are interested in working across issue areas.

3. **ADVOCACY to Develop and Change Policies and Laws**
   Working for policy change and human rights legislation can bring human rights to your city, country, or state.

Five Ways to Include Human Rights in Your Work

1. Begin using a human rights language and framework. For example: *"health is a human right"* or *"you have a right to an adequate standard of living."*

2. Offer a copy of the Universal Declaration of Human Rights (UDHR) to your board of directors, employer, employees, philanthropists, clients, colleagues, friends, and associates.

3. Learn which human rights treaties address the issues you care about. Find out whether the US has ratified these treaties and learn about the reports that the

government and non-governmental organizations have provided to the United Nations.[6]

4. Connect with a human rights organization and/or human rights centers at universities in your community and find out what they are doing locally.

5. Ask local human rights organizations (such as a local chapter of Amnesty International) for support, including a briefing or training on the relevance of human rights to the issues you care about. Many jurisdictions put requirements for funding into the resolution or ordinance or were funded locally by women's funds.

What Are Human Rights Treaties?

Also known as conventions, treaties are international documents that describe and protect human rights and explain the steps governments must take to enforce these standards. Governments must agree to follow treaties' provisions. These are different from declarations, such as the Universal Declaration of Human Rights (UDHR), which is not legally binding, though they serve to define and set standards for human rights. Most human rights treaties emerge from the United Nations. Regional human rights treaties, such as the American Convention on Human Rights, emerge from regional organizations, such as the Inter-American Human Rights Commission.

In 1948, members of the United Nations unanimously adopted the Universal Declaration of Human Rights (UDHR). The United Nations has subsequently drafted a number of treaties—including CEDAW and the Convention on the Elimination of all forms of Racial Discrimination (CERD)—with the purpose of clarifying and enforcing the principles of the UDHR and addressing the barriers to human rights faced by certain groups. Treaties are legally binding within a nation if ratified by that nation's government.

---

6   For complete list of US ratified human rights treaties see: https://tbinternet.ohchr.org/_layouts/15/TreatyBodyExternal/Treaty.aspx?CountryID=187&Lang=EN

Who Is Responsible for Human Rights?

- Ultimately, the responsibility to make human rights a reality lies with all of us. Although human rights treaties have traditionally held only governments accountable for their action and inaction, the responsibility to uphold human rights extends equally to individuals, organizations, corporations, governments, and other institutions.

- At times, in collaboration with governments, community-based organizations and advocates have educated the public about human rights and advocated for policies that implement human rights.

Why Is CEDAW Important?

CEDAW is an international bill of rights that outlines human rights through the lens of barriers and discrimination faced by women and girls, because of their gender.

CEDAW provides the most comprehensive definition of discrimination against women and girls as:

... Any distinction, exclusion, or restriction made on the basis of sex that has the effect or purpose of impairing or nullifying the recognition, enjoyment, or exercise by women, irrespective of their marital status, on a basis or equality of men and women, of human rights and fundamental freedoms in the political, economic, social, cultural, civil or any other field.

CEDAW has 23 Articles that cover the definition of discrimination, areas of discrimination such as in employment, education, political life, and how the treaty should work when ratified. At a later stage of the treaty, General Recommendations are issued in

CEDAW General Recommendation 37 on the Gender-related dimensions of disaster Risk Reduction in a Changing Climate

Large urban areas and megacities, particularly those in low-income countries located in coastal areas, are increasingly being exposed to climate-related risks. This exposure has widespread negative impacts on health, livelihoods, and assets with urban women, especially in the low-income countries, being disproportionately affected.

order to update and interpret the treaty relevant to current times. For example, the definition expands to include how gender-based violence disproportionately affects women.

CEDAW also asserts that women experience discrimination in all spheres, within families, communities, and government entities. For women and girls to enjoy full human rights, discriminatory barriers must be eliminated, and CEDAW ensures that governments are working toward protecting, respecting, and fulfilling the rights of women and girls in all their diversity.

CEDAW provides a comprehensive description of the human rights of women, including the right to:

- Health, including reproductive rights
- Family
- Education
- Work
- An adequate standard of living
- Access to decision-making
- Freedom from violence
- Bodily integrity
- Marriage
- Citizenship
- Political participation

CEDAW General Recommendation 24; Article 12 on health

31.c [States parties should] prioritize the prevention of unwanted pregnancy through family planning and sex education and reduce maternal mortality rates through safe motherhood services and prenatal assistance. When possible, legislation criminalizing abortion should be amended, in order to withdraw punitive measures imposed on women who undergo abortion.

Ratification and Implementation

RATIFICATION means that a government has taken steps to hold themselves legally obligated to the conditions of a treaty.

IMPLEMENTATION means enforcing a law or treaty that has been passed.

How can the US ratify a treaty?

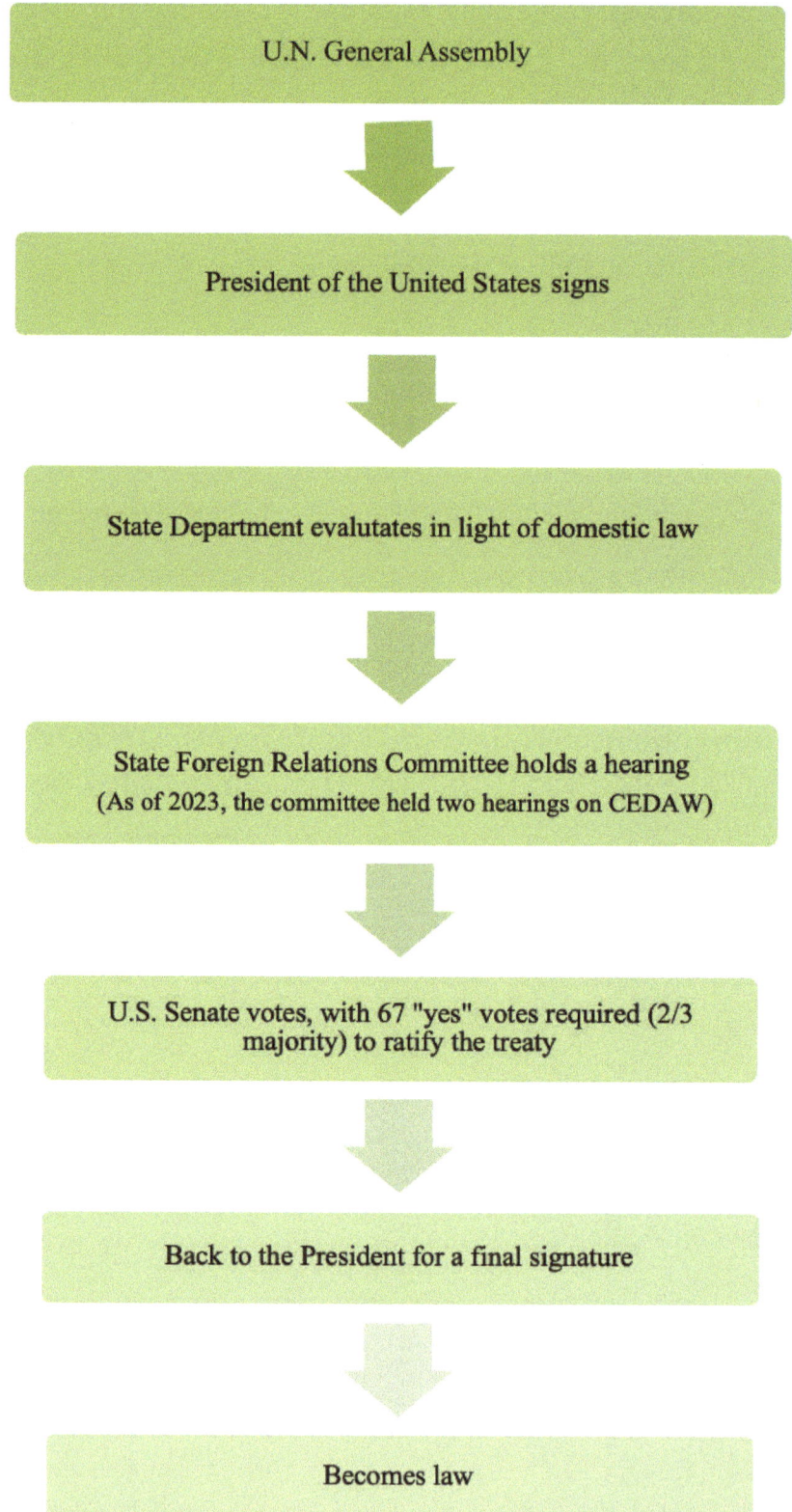

U.N. General Assembly

↓

President of the United States signs

↓

State Department evalutates in light of domestic law

↓

State Foreign Relations Committee holds a hearing
(As of 2023, the committee held two hearings on CEDAW)

↓

U.S. Senate votes, with 67 "yes" votes required (2/3 majority) to ratify the treaty

↓

Back to the President for a final signature

↓

Becomes law

Why Is Local Implementation of Human Rights Treaties Important?

The local ratification and implementation of human rights treaties bring international human rights standards into our communities, thereby allowing for development of proactive legislation. Local implementation ensures that such treaties will, in fact, improve the lives of communities for the long term.

Ratification in our cities, counties, and states sends a strong message to elected federal officials, and to the president that national ratification and implementation are important to their constituencies. Enforcing human rights standards locally connects us to the global human rights movements and provides us with mechanisms to adopt successful strategies and best practices in the United States.

National Strategy on Gender Equity and Equality. The White House 2021.

We will continue to support the Equal Rights Amendment which would make gender equality explicit in the U.S. Constitution as well as the ratification of the Convention on the Elimination of All forms of Discrimination Against Women...

What Are Human Rights with a Gender Perspective?

Focusing on gender means examining ways that people are treated differently and assigned inequitable roles, responsibilities, and opportunities based on the social construction of physical (or biological) sex. The role of gender still functions to subordinate and discriminate against women to the detriment of their full enjoyment of all human rights. Gender-based discrimination affects individual relationships, institutions, and communities.

Our identities and experiences such as but not limited to race, class, sexual

CEDAW General Recommendation 35 on violence against women

States parties should report on all forms of gender-based violence, and such reports should include all available data on the incidence of each form of violence and on the effects of such violence on the women who are victims.

orientation, age, ability, and immigrant status—determine how we experience gender-based discrimination. The power differences assigned to gender, race, age, sexual orientation, class, ability, and other aspects of identify mitigate our ability to exercise human rights. Without fully addressing the multiple and interconnected identities of a person or community, we cannot ensure the enjoyment of human rights. Therefore, we cannot consider gender in isolation from other identities.

In the United States, women and girls experience a range of human rights violations such as inadequate living standards, lack of access to health care, employment discrimination, gender-based education, and violence within their families, communities, and governments.

BUILDING YOUR COALITION

For Discussion

- How do you think you can contribute to the implementation of CEDAW where you live?

- Can you name five reasons to work together with partner organizations?

- Can you name some groups or people to contact about building a coalition that you usually may not work with such as faith-based groups, youth, or influencers?

- What are some difficulties and strengths of working with government agencies? Community-based organizations?

First Steps

The first step in our planning process is to create a planning structure that will guide decisions and tasks for advancing CEDAW in your local community. The structure should be determined by the individuals and organizations working on local implementation.

Building coalitions is an integral component of implementation and engaging many people in this ongoing process will ensure that your efforts will be long-lasting and relevant. Those most impacted by the issues must be part of the leadership. A collaborative model will best reflect the intersection of people's identities and experiences and will ensure that CEDAW implementation reflects the needs of each community.

Bringing together community support and leadership that is informed, diverse, and committed means presenting numerous ways to get involved. In the long run, giving time to this stage will lead to a well-coordinated, broadly supported, and consequently more effective implementation effort.

In this section, we offer recommendations for questions that might arise in the beginning stages. We also provide specific examples from our experience in San Francisco (see the *San Francisco* text boxes) to help advance and define your objectives.

Community Involvement

By creating numerous levels of involvement in a coalition, you will be able to include people with varying resources and time. We found the following three tiers of involvement to be most effective:

Take the lead as a *partner organization*. Partners have the largest stake and make the biggest commitment of time, money, and resources to the effort. They are the key decision-makers on an ongoing basis. It is best to have a maximum of five partner organizations to maintain clear communication and accountability.

Join the *community task force*. Task force members hold regular meetings and make strategic decisions along with the lead partners, play a key role in organizing public hearings and other events, speak publicly about CEDAW, and run community trainings. This is an action-based coalition made up of community leaders.

Serve as *supporting organizations and individuals*. Community supporters endorse the efforts of the partners and task force and communicate with their constituencies about CEDAW. They may act as spokespeople in their communities, provide forums for task force members to speak about CEDAW, write newsletter articles, or simply lend their names to your effort.

Task Force Recommended Within Ordinance

Honolulu CEDAW ordinance 2015

d.1 A CEDAW task force is hereby established. The task force shall report to the mayor and the committee. The committee shall provide administrative support for the task force. The CEDAW task force shall consist of ten members. The members of the task force shall be as follows: a staff member from the mayor's office knowledgeable about the city's budget, to be designated by the mayor; The director of the department of human resources or her or his designee; The chair of the council or her or his designee; The Chair of the committee or her or his designee; and Six members from the community to be appointed by the committee.

Identifying Partner Organizations

Pittsburgh city press conference with coalition members

Partners must have the institutional strength and commitment to be part of a cutting-edge process. They must have a vision and a stake in making it happen. The criteria to identify partnership organizations mean they are:

- Able to devote time, money, and resources (including personnel)
- Relatively equal and significant stake, investment, and commitment
- Able to make key decisions weekly and on an ongoing basis
- Connected to or have deep knowledge of community concerns and priorities
- Able to disagree without jeopardizing the process
- Capable of mutual trust with other partners (or desire to create that trust)

How Do Partners Share the Work?

One or more of the partner organizations should take the lead in your CEDAW effort. It is important to decide which group(s) will act as the lead, or information clearinghouse, to maintain accountability. If possible, two organizations should share the lead, which means sharing the work.

San Francisco 1998

WILD for Human Rights sought partnership with Amnesty International, the Women's Foundation, La Casa de las Madres, and the Commission on the Status of Women. Amnesty International provided a large constituency, leadership for national ratification, and credibility as a global human rights organization. The Women's Foundation, a part of the philanthropic community, provided access to community organizations, an interest in policymaking, and credibility. La Casa de las Madres, a direct service provider for survivors of domestic violence, worked with one of the populations directly impacted by the ordinance. The Commission on the Status of Women was an ally inside city government that could move toward implementation. All these organizations engaged in developing key strategies.

WiLD for Human Rights offered vision and expertise about the human rights of women and girls in the United States. WILD for Human Rights spearheaded the process by setting meeting agendas and schedules, advancing communications, leading the administrative work, fundraising, developing media contacts, and offering trainings.

Building a Community Task Force

Task force members participate in monthly meetings, play a key role in organizing public hearings and other events, and run community trainings. This is an action-based coalition made up of community leaders.

How Do You Build a Community Task Force?

1. Identify and contact people who are making decisions (e.g., executive directors, board members, city officials) in programs and organizations that serve women and girls or work against gender discrimination. Schedule one-on-one meetings with them to discuss CEDAW and examine its relevance to their work.

2. Design a workshop that addresses the questions:
   a) Why human rights?
   b) What is CEDAW?
   c) How is it relevant to our community and work?
   The introductory section, "What Is Cities for CEDAW?," of this manual offers a few answers to these questions. Prepare to hold ongoing trainings for your task force.

3. Contact community groups. Offer them ways to support the effort and invite them and key decision-makers to a workshop. If communicating through letter or email, follow up with a phone call.

4. Once the group or organization has attended a workshop, invite them to join the task force.

Washington DC CEDAW ordinance 2023

J. Expenses for operation of the Commission shall be met by such appropriations as made by City council in accordance with the budget prepared by the Commission and submitted to City council. Expenses may also be met by contributions from outside sources…185.03 To implement CEDAW and eliminate discrimination against women and girls, selected city departments, programs, policies, and private entities to the extent permitted by law shall develop a Departmental Action Plan.

5. Based on need and your strategic timeline, form ad hoc subcommittees to do outreach, media work, event planning, and training.

6. Identify what skills and information task force members need to be most effective (e.g., media advocacy, city politics, public speaking) and design ongoing trainings for the task force.

What Are the Criteria for Task Force Members?

- Acknowledge human rights for all people
- Participated in a CEDAW workshop
- Able to meet monthly for decision-making meeting
- Dedicated to the goals of the task force
- Connected to a community that will be directly impacted by the ordinance
- Represent the wide diversity of stakeholders by age, race and ethnicity, religion, socio-economic and cultural status, and gender identity, among others

San Francisco 1998

An important element of our work to implement CEDAW in San Francisco was to develop a strong coalition of government, community-based, and public-interest organizations to support education and advocacy efforts. This task force provided guidance and support (trainings, outreach, public hearing planning, and education) and worked on the process of drafting and passing a city ordinance to implement CEDAW. Any individuals or groups who attended a monthly CEDAW workshop could choose to join this task force.

How Do You Ensure Diverse Leadership?

An ideal coalition represents your community's diversity as well as a variety of skills and knowledge. Your coalition might include:

- Direct service providers

- Youth

- Community members and institutions that have demonstrated a good analysis of race, immigration-status, ethnicity, sexual orientation, age, ability, and class, and who represent such diversity

- Individuals and groups with a primary interest in improving the lives of women and girls

- Faith-based community groups and individuals

- Individuals and groups whose lives are directly impacted

- Individuals who are primary decision-makers in their communities

- Individuals and organizations with legal and policy expertise and experience, especially in human rights and civil rights law

- Individuals who are closely tied to city politics and the mayor's office

- Strategic thinkers

- Communications experts

- Media and Communications experts

Toledo Ohio CEDAW ordinance 2022

Summary Background c. There is a continued need for the City of Toledo to protect the human rights of women and girls by addressing discrimination … Further, the City of Toledo will focus on the issues affecting women and girls of ethnic and racial minorities, women and girls in poverty; women and girls with disability; women and girls in the LGBTIQ+ community; and women and girls who are immigrants, asylees, and refugees.

Suggested Steps to Form Coalitions

1. **Orientation**

   Provide substantial information about positions and roles as well as information about key organization and issues to all task force members. Offer a complete list of responsibilities and expectations. Identify one or two people they can speak to about problems they experience with the coalition or other members.

2. **Ongoing Training**

   Provide human rights and intersectional analysis training for all the task force members as part of a regular meeting schedule. Provide initial and ongoing training in leadership skills, including public speaking, strategy, advocacy, facilitation, and decision-making.

3. **Meetings**

   Be sensitive about meeting and workshop times. It may be difficult for working women and women with children to meet during weekdays or at other times. Ask about members' schedules and time constraints.

4. **Childcare and Transportation**

   Assume that you will need to provide childcare during your meetings and other events. Hold meetings in locations that are easily accessible to public transportation. Foster an organizational commitment to reimburse or provide stipends to low-income women and youth.

5. **Communication**

   Cultural difference often includes different communication styles. Create facilitation and meeting structures (e.g., ground rules for discussion) that ensure that all voices are heard and that there is space for anecdotes, conflict resolution, and relationship building.

6. **Decision-making**

   Avoid the oversight of assuming that the interest of the "majority" is that of the entire group, particularly when identifying which priority issues to work on. Build decision-making structures that encourage participation.

Young Women and Leadership

By including young woman in every step of the process, you will ensure that their needs are addressed and their strengths are utilized. Below are steps for successfully involving young women in the decision-making process.

1. **Orientation**

   Provide background information on the position you are asking young women to fill, as well as information about key organizations and issues. Offer a complete list of responsibilities and expectations and identify one or two people to whom young women can bring concerns or suggestions about their experience.

2. **Ongoing Training**

   Provide initial and ongoing training in leadership skills such as public speaking, human rights, facilitation, decision-making, and strategic planning.

3. **Visible Leadership**

   Offer young women leadership roles in project design and implementation. Trust them to be the experts on their own communities and issues. Provide public speaking opportunities and ask them to chair or facilitate meetings. Create a meeting structure that encourages everyone to speak. Integrate young women into all areas of decision-making, not just those issues affecting young people, while holding them accountable for leadership follow-through.

4. **Outreach with Peer Leadership**

   Involve young women in the recruitment of new youth participants. They will know how to reach out to other young women.

5. **Train Adults**

   Train adults on how to respectfully interact with young women without being patronizing. Describe a clear line of supervision or support, so that everyone knows who is responsible for providing feedback to young women. Address sexual harassment as something that happens more frequently to young women. Check back with young women to see that the coalition's environment is comfortable for them.

6. **Intergenerational Partners**

   Foster structured, one-on-one relationships between young women and adults. Promote an atmosphere that is open to two-way learning and be aware that young women will often have new perspectives.

7. **Peer Support**

Involve two or more young women in the work of the coalition to help them to feel supported and confident in their positions.

8. **Accommodate**

Respect young women's needs to prioritize commitments such as education, social life, and family, particularly in the case of young mothers. Recognize young women's financial and transportation constraints while ensuring that they remain responsible for their commitments.

9. **Compensation**

Foster an organizational or governmental commitment to compensate young women for their work.

10. **Create Space**

Create physical and practical space to prevent marginalization of young women's voices and projects. Place young women on meeting agendas. Create office space for their work.

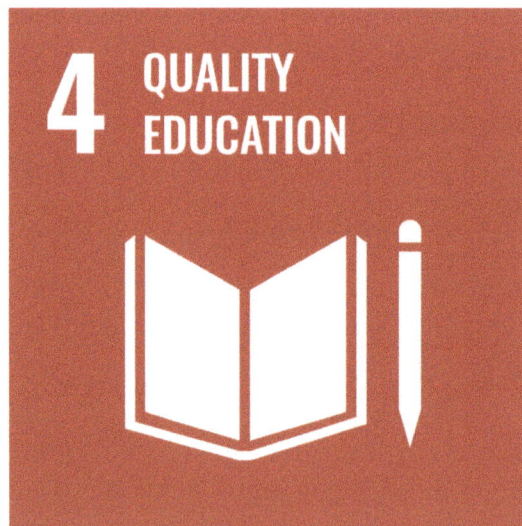

San Francisco 1998

Although a number of young women were members of the task force, the partner organizations felt that extra effort was needed to ensure that young women were effectively included in strategy development and not relegated to administrative work. We wanted young women to be valued contributors for a variety of reasons.

First, since the San Francisco CEDAW Ordinance would impact young women and girls, we believed that their voices had to be part of the decision-making process. More importantly, young women can make valuable contributions about both strategy and substantive aspects of the law. The task force ensured that young women held decision-making positions and that their contributions were encouraged and respected. In addition, all task force members were expected to assist with administrative work.

When organizing the public hearing in San Francisco, the youth on the task force played a central role in identifying and confirming speakers and coordinating the logistics. At the hearing, one young woman gave testimony about her experience with sexual harassment in a local high school, and one of the youngest members of the task force was one of the two community members who served as an expert panelist. Young women were involved in the development of public hearings and training materials. They worked on advocacy and outreach and held vital roles during the implementation stages.

Maintaining a Strong Task Force

Maintaining a strong task force requires clarifying structure, purpose, financing, and commitment. Consider the following questions along with your partners and task force coalition:

- How can city officials and coalitions work together to form a task force?

- Why is it important to build broad-based community support for local CEDAW legislation? Why is public support important?

- What would make it easy for people to join?

- How should internal decisions be made?

- What are the different roles and who would be best suited to fulfill each one? How will you assign tasks and set up a structure for accountability? Do you want to create and document these agreements in writing?

- For each member of the task force: What is your stake in doing this work? How will you or your community benefit? Why are you here?

- What is the process for incorporating new members and making sure they are immediately updated on the status of work?

- Would you like the task force to exist after your implementation effort is successful? If so, for what purpose? How will you formalize a process of continued interaction (e.g., meetings, community outreach, and similar activities)?

- How can you fund a task force and what is the role of city financing?

Potential Topics for Ongoing Task Force Trainings and Discussion

1. How does the task force address issues based on gender, race, class, age, sexual orientation, ability, religion, nationality, and other aspects of identity, in both the structure and process?

2. How does your city operate? Where are the pressures and points of power? How does an ordinance pass locally?

3. What media source reaches diverse constituencies in your communities?

4. What skills do you need to make the best decisions?

5. What communities are not currently represented and what should be put in place to include them?

San Francisco 1998

We made it a priority to develop strong working relationships among all task force members because the task force included community members from a variety of backgrounds as well as representatives from both government and community-based organizations. The tension between government and community groups proved to be the most significant. We found that this tension gave us advance warning about issues that could be contentious, and we were then able to formulate responses and/or revise our policies to have a smooth process. As a result of our public/private partnership, we discussed the most acrimonious issues prior to meeting with groups outside our coalition. Thus, we were ultimately able to use internal conflict resolution processes to strengthen our coalition's presentation.

Once the community task force was formed and had established a workshop to continue recruiting new members, the next step was to maintain unity and effectiveness within the coalition. We held monthly meetings to evaluate strategy on CEDAW education and implementation, plan CEDAW trainings, discuss outreach to communities, and plan a public hearing. These meetings provided regular interaction between task force members, allowing us to develop relationships, learn about different activities and organizations around the city, and become comfortable with the various working styles that we would encounter in our pursuit of CEDAW implementation.

Working in a Coalition

The best strategy is to be prepared for miscommunication and to use mutual respect as an overarching goal.

When working in coalition with community-based organizations and government agencies, both challenges and strengths will emerge as these groups join their mandates and constituencies. Below are a few guidelines for collaboration.

Tips for Community-based Organizations That Are Working Together

1. The work of one group or type of organization (e.g., direct service, policy, litigation, etc.) is not more important than that of another. We all have a part in strengthening human rights. It is critical to incorporate groups that represent various approaches.

2. Strategically decide who should have a prominent role at any given time; allow for the roles to shift over time.

3. Every meeting (internal and external) should include someone who is thoroughly knowledgeable about CEDAW and understands the possibilities for local, practical applications of CEDAW.

Tips for Working With Government Agencies

1. Remember that the strength of your coalition is based on the number and diversity of people you represent. Constituencies can attend events, such as public hearings, to demonstrate your strength.

2. The government is there to serve you and those you represent; the city is working for you. Keep this in mind particularly when negotiating ordinance language. The size of your constituency will again become relevant.

3. Government commissions, in particular, are in a unique position to be a broker between public-interest groups and government. CEDAW can also bolster women's commissions' positions in government because it strengthens the city's mandate to redress gender discrimination.

4. Ensuring representatives from your organizations or community in government positions, for example on commissions, will create a long-term presence in the city.

A Note About Working With the Private Sector

The private sector is playing an increasingly large role in people's lives. You may want to consider doing outreach, including workshops, for local businesses or inviting representatives to join your task force. Chances are that, as with governments, community groups and for-profit corporations will not be familiar with each other's work and will need to take time to become more knowledgeable. Seek out individuals in business who have a strong tie to community work. Since most multinational corporations negatively impact the lives of women in the US and globally, we urge you to make decisions wisely via extensive research. In San Francisco, there was no corporate involvement. However, the small business community did participate, particularly women-owned businesses.

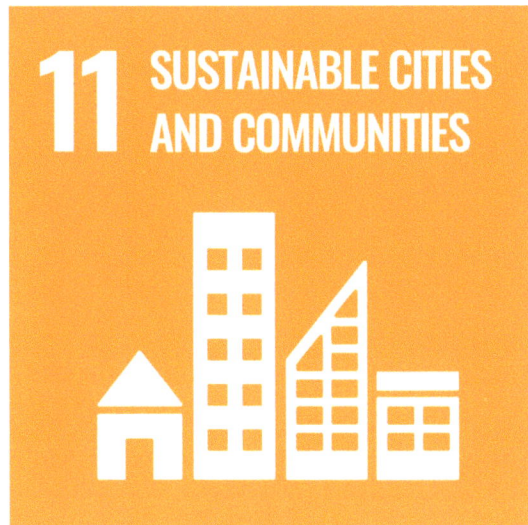

Government Efforts For Implementation

Gavin Newsom, former mayor of San Francisco, former county supervisor, and current governor of California, speaks out for CEDAW

This section is directed to public officials, government offices, and city commissions that have an interest in working on local implementation but would also like more information. This section will provide suggestions for government bodies that are interested in collaborating with community-based and public-interest organizations to achieve your goals.

Why Should Government Groups Pursue Human Rights Implementation?

Much of the government, like many other sectors, tends to be fragmented. A city such as San Francisco (population: 800,000) has approximately 64 city departments and commissions that act with individual mandates and separate budgets and leadership, albeit under the mayor's office. A human rights framework provides a lens through which different departments can view their work as part of a whole. CEDAW provides a gender lens as part of a larger, common vision that brings principles of international human rights to your city. Through this process, you will learn how to meaningfully address the needs of women and girls. Women's commissions are often well-positioned to take a lead role, bring in other government entities, and provide access to city decision-makers who can effect change.

San Diego County CEDAW ordinance 2022.

F1. Housing and homelessness: The county shall take appropriate and timely measure to ensure equitable access to affordable, permanent housing options for women and girls … Section 3A. The Chief Administrative officer shall be responsible for coordinating and directing the completion of an intersectional gender analysis of the entire county, including county departments, offices, programs, boards, commissions, and other operation units.

Why Partner With Community-based Organizations?

Change at the government level occurs slowly. Points of collaboration with community groups provide creativity and offer different models of work. Partnering brings credibility to the process and ensures that the work is grounded to the needs of the community. To have credibility, to make sure programs relate to community needs, and to carry out effective actions, you need the backing of non-governmental organizations and their constituencies. Government can play a unique role in collaboration by convening people for discussion and action in official and semi-official forums.

Tips for Government Groups Working With Community-based Organizations

1. Let the community know you are there to support them and their needs.

2. Become familiar with the basic substance of their work. For example, what are the issues that groups are pursuing? Through research and by attending local events, you can become familiar with the ideas and innovations of community groups.

3. Gain an understanding of how community-based organizations function (e.g., how they are funded).

4. Not every community group is policy-oriented or understands the workings of city government. This may be a learning process for all those involved. If community groups understand government—not just the mechanisms, but who the important staff and aides are—they can use government channels more effectively. Government members of a community task force may want to consider providing this training.

5. Know where your accountability lies. Communities are both your allies and your conscience.

Developing a CEDAW Workshop

Training community members about human rights is an integral part of a strategy to improve the lives of women and girls. For CEDAW to have a concrete impact, it is important to build a constituency of advocates and activists who understand the document and can apply its principles to their work. The grassroots adoption of the tenets of human rights must occur before CEDAW can be used as the blueprint for meaningful changes in government policies. You can begin the implementation process by leading monthly workshops on CEDAW for local activists, educators, community organizers, and city officials.

This section offers a summary of workshop goals and recommendations for planning and content. It also includes a case study from San Francisco and a sample workshop agenda.

What Are Possible Goals for Workshops?

1. To educate NGO leaders, academics, researchers, individual community members, and city officials about human rights and CEDAW.

2. To convene groups and individuals who can strategize about ways to integrate the values and principles of CEDAW on a local level.

3. To prepare the task force members and other affiliate groups to effectively promote the CEDAW process and testify at public hearings.

4. To provide an entry point for task force participation.

5. To gather information about how CEDAW could improve the lives of women and girls through exercises and documentation.

6. To mobilize the media and influencers on social media.

Recommendations for Workshops

Structure

- Reserve time at each task force meeting for the trainers to debrief about that month's workshop to share what did and did not work.

- Through a "training of trainers," prepare a team of people from a variety of backgrounds to lead the workshops.

- Create a monthly schedule that identifies dates and trainers for each workshop.

- Conduct workshops regularly (monthly or bi-monthly) to bring new people into your task force.

- Invite a diverse range of participants including direct service workers, community-based organizations, policy and advocacy groups, and government staff to attend the workshops.

- Go out into the community to do workshops (e.g., for the entire staff of an organization, at a community center, or a local college). This may mean doing workshops more frequently.

- Ensure attendance through RSVPs and direct outreach. A workshop for twelve is more productive and livelier than a workshop for two.

- After the workshop, follow up with people and organizations that attended.

Send them information about task force meetings, public hearings, and advocacy opportunities.

- Provide issue-focused workshop (e.g., women's health and CEDAW), but always make sure that you relate the issues to other conditions that impact women's lives (e.g., how health is related to violence, economics, education, and political participation).

Content

- Before presenting workshops or building a task force, it is important to be familiar with CEDAW and human rights. See the "What Is Cities for CEDAW?" section of this workbook for more information.

- Identify your audience and outline effective, audience-specific messages. You may want to develop two or three models for specific audiences (e.g., youth, businesswomen) and different venues (e.g., shorter/longer time, location).

- Be realistic about treaty implementation. Do not make promises about CEDAW or about what your government cannot or will not deliver.

- Present the benefits and limitations of the human rights framework.

- Create interactive exercises that combine information with hands-on learning.

- Always connect the content to issues currently faced by the community. Use examples from daily, local news sources or community organizations to make real-life connections to CEDAW (e.g., bring newspaper or magazine articles to illustrate your points). Ask participants to share information about issues in their communities.

- Before a workshop, create suggestions for concrete actions for the participants.

- Make time to access the participants' interests, skills, and contacts.

San Francisco 1998

Through the coordination of WILD for Human Rights, the task force offered monthly workshops on CEDAW to advocates and community organizations serving women and girls. A minimum of two task force members facilitated each four-hour workshop. To recruit workshop participants, WILD for Human Rights distributed a mailing to individuals and organizations from the partner organizations' mailing lists. The mailing included a brief description of CEDAW and a statement about the task force on the letterhead of the Commission on the Status of Women. It also included a form that asked for individual or organizational endorsement, and it gauged their interest in attending a free CEDAW workshop.

Interested individuals returned the form to WILD for Human Rights, and staff members then called them and signed them up for the appropriate workshops. We found that several people were interested in attending but were unable to attend on weekdays. In response, the task force began to offer Saturday workshops.

For our very first workshop, WILD for Human Rights brought together twenty-four women from the Bay Area for a two-day training. The participants were working in three issue areas: violence, economic justice, and health. The workshop attendees became the first task force members. The two primary organizing questions for this training were:

1. How does CEDAW relate to our lives, work, and communities?
2. How do we make policy or impact existing policy based on international human rights standards?

Members of the task force who were familiar with CEDAW and had done similar workshops in the past facilitated the initial workshops. However, it soon became clear that the burden of preparing the agenda and handouts, confirming the attendance of participants, and coordinating the four-hour workshop fell on the same people every month. In response, we decided to have a training of trainers.

The training of trainers was an extensive, eight-hour training for members of the task force facilitated by WILD for Human Rights. At the end of the training of trainers, the trainees reviewed the upcoming schedule of workshops and signed up in pairs to facilitate at least one of these workshops. Each pair was responsible for creating an agenda and selecting handouts. The workshop was held in the shared offices of the Women's Foundation and WILD for Human Rights. WILD for Human Rights continued to be responsible for confirming attendance and ordering food.

Attendance at each workshop ranged from two to fifteen people, with an average of six participants. The participants were predominantly women from local organizations that served women and girls, attorneys, union members, people involved in the city government, and activists involved in several issue areas ranging from immigrant rights to the rights of sex workers.

While the style of the workshops and the agenda depended largely on the facilitators and the audience, they almost always began with an exercise that focused on the participants' personal experiences with human rights violations and their knowledge of human rights. A sample agenda is included below.

The second section of the workshops included an overview of human rights instruments, the national human rights movement, and the global women's human rights movement. Participants learned about:

- The structure of the United Nations
- The origins of the women's human rights movement
- The United Nations Decade for Women
- United Nations conference and other treaties that impact the lives of women and girls

The next part of the workshops focused on CEDAW, including the historical background of the treaty, and information about the United States involvement in the writing and signing of the Convention. Workshop facilitators went through each article in the treaty and asked participants to identify its relevance to the local community. General topics such as enforceability and the role of the United Nations CEDAW committee were also covered. The participants were able to reflect on the convention and discuss how the articles speak to problems in the US such as welfare reform, anti-affirmative action measures, and resistance to same-sex marriage.

The workshops often concluded with a discussion about the potential relevance of CEDAW to the lives and work of the participants. The trainers encouraged participants to think about how to implement the languages and values of CEDAW in their current work communities. Strategies for national ratification as well as information about the local implementation process were shared with participants. All participants were encouraged to join the task force.

The monthly CEDAW workshops helped push forward the local process in two key ways:

1. Participants joined the task force and became members, bringing new skills or specialized knowledge to the group.
2. The workshops served as a platform for community members about CEDAW and its possible applications. Because many of the participants came from community-based organizations, the task force gained support and/or sponsorship for the public hearing.

Challenges

We encountered a number of challenges when providing CEDAW workshops in San Francisco. They are listed here to help you anticipate similar challenges.

- Opposition by anti-human rights groups
- Outreach: Identifying individuals and groups to attend the workshops
- Canceling workshops due to lack of interest or attendance by fewer than three people

- Finding time for training teams to plan their agendas and workshop format

- Ensuring that people trained to lead workshops actually did so

- Covering a substantial amount of material in a four-hour workshop

- Following up with workshop participants

- Financing mobilization

- Moving from city resolution to ordinance

Suggestions for Addressing Challenges

1. Study the experiences of opposition groups and prepare for countermeasures such as press releases and education programs addressing the opposing points of views.

2. Review experiences of other jurisdictions for lessons learned about how to build on existing declarations, resolutions, and other ordinances.

3. Draw on the task force members and your community base to recruit workshop participants.

4. Find convenient times to hold the workshops for working people, including evenings and weekends. Be flexible about the number and timing of workshops.

5. Establish a system of accountability for workshop planning. You may want to ask one or two people from a partner organization to take responsibility for scheduling and planning workshops. Their responsibilities would include following up with people who have been trained to lead workshops, creating the workshop schedule, and keeping track of how many people plan to attend the workshops.

6. Set up a database of workshop participants that will help you follow up with them.

7. Anticipate costs and plan how to mobilize local resources that can sustain momentum.

Working Toward Change

cities for cedaw

For Discussion

- Can you list five government officials to contact?
- Have you had experience passing resolutions or ordinances?
- What kinds of public hearings work best in your community?
- Do you have contacts with other cities where CEDAW has been passed?

Communities can use policy changes informed by the principles of human rights in local schools, membership organizations, and governments to hold these and other institutions accountable to human rights standards. Building relationships, doing public education, and making policy changes are all aspects of implementation that make rights a reality. There are many creative ways to bring the idea of the human rights framework into social change efforts in your local communities. Your goals, and the context in which you are working, will determine your implementation strategy. This section offers some suggestions based on our strengths and experiences in San Francisco.

Meeting With Public Officials

Why Are Meetings With Public Officials Important?

Meetings with public officials are necessary to determine who your allies are, and to identify other relevant or opposing policies or legislation. Through meetings, you can collaborate and move forward with public officials who share your ideals and dialogues with those who do not.

How Can We Identify Allies?

Members of your task force who work closely with or are part of the government will be the best source for contacts. If none of your organizers have government contacts, you will want to meet with the heads of government commissions to discuss CEDAW and attend meetings of key commissions to determine which ones might pass supporting resolutions. (In San Francisco, eight commissions passed resolutions prior to the public hearing.) You may also want to organize a presentation for your women's commission, human rights commission, or civil rights commission.

For the governing body of your city (e.g., city council), you can also get voting records from the previous year's meetings to determine which officials are most likely to support your work. Eventually, you will want to include government representatives on your task force or find allies inside government agencies (e.g., the women's commission).

Santa Clara CEDAW Pledge

The women's commission in Santa Clara County used a CEDAW pledge campaign to ensure that political leaders and city council members signed a commitment to support CEDAW. The pledge is an effective measure to use before a vote to hold signatories accountable.

Even though you will make many contacts through your task force and government partners, the time will almost certainly come when you must meet with a government official you do not know.

Checklist for Meeting With New Government Officials

- Do your homework on who they are and what they care about. Tailor your meetings to highlight the relationship between your work and their interests.

- Contact them through email when asking for a meeting, describing why you want a meeting and whom you represent.

- Call to follow up and make an appointment. Call again the day before the meeting to confirm.

- Before the meeting, create an agenda that addresses what you want from that person specifically. Prepare to say what you need from them in fifteen minutes (or calculate for half the time allotted, since they may be pulled out of the meeting). What you want depends on where you are in the process.

- If you bring a large constituency, not more than two to three people should speak. Coordinate talking points for each speaker ahead of time. Others can speak when necessary.

- Be specific and clear. Ask for what you want as politely as possible.

- If the person you meet with will not give you a definite answer about whether they support you (i.e., how they will vote), make sure to ask, "When can we expect a decision to be made?" A definite answer is what you need.

- Pay attention to the words and body language of their staff, particularly their most influential aides. In legislators' offices, aides will follow up with you, and they are the people you should stay in touch with. Get business cards.

- Immediately after the meeting, write a thank-you letter that reiterates promises for agreements made in the meeting.

- If you did not get commitments, follow up with a phone call or letter in about a week.

When Meeting With Government Officials

- Be direct but not abrupt.

- Always know your bottom line and how much you are willing to negotiate.

- If you do not know something, admit it and offer to research only if you have the capacity.

- If you promise something, deliver it.

- Offer a brief list or single page of information that reflects your talking points.

- Dress professionally.

- Be courteous.

- Remember who you are representing and are accountable to.

What Should We Know Before Meeting With Someone to Ask for Their Support?

1. What is their relationship to other government officials?

2. Are they in a leadership position?

3. What issue areas are they interested in professionally?

4. What are the possible connections among these interests and CEDAW?

5. How have they voted on related issues?

6. What are their personal interests?

7. What communities are they part of or have an affinity for?

8. Do you know anyone in common?

9. With what social and religious institutions are they associated?

10. Do they have school-age children?

11. What did they do before they ran for office?

What Should We Ask for?

You may be asking for their vote, presence at a meeting, a call to the mayor, to urge budget changes, or to add their name to a list of supporters. What you ask for depends specifically on what you are trying to accomplish at that point in time. In general, you are usually seeking a long-term relationship.

Passing a Resolution

What Is a Resolution?

A resolution is a declaration about what a city's elected leadership wants to say or see happen. It is not legally binding, but it will tell you where officials stand. A resolution is a very important first step for several reasons:

- Passing a resolution is a first step toward passing an ordinance, providing a foundation on which to build.

- Because a resolution is not legally binding—although it includes a philosophical commitment and does not have to involve a monetary commitment—it is not too threatening for opponents.

- Local resolutions send a message to the national government, especially the US Senate, about how people feel about CEDAW and how important national ratification is.

Who Writes a Resolution?

The process differs by locale, but a government body drafts the language of a resolution to be approved by the city council, the county board of supervisors, or state legislature. The resolution is usually introduced by an individual city council member and is drafted by their aides and legal staff. Community-based and public interest organizations can influence the process but do not actually write the text. You will want to research whether the legislator has done work on women's rights or human rights in the past and whether they have the credibility and integrity to represent a resolution on CEDAW.

City departments and commissions can strengthen the foundation for a resolution by passing department-specific internal resolutions. You may want to obtain a list or minutes of all commission meetings during a three-month period and identify those you want to work with to pass resolutions. Eventually, you will need to attend these commission meetings and make public comments encouraging the passage of a resolution on CEDAW. It is important to include a variety of commissions in this process, not just those that are staffed by greater numbers of women. Choose commissions carefully to recognize their work on relevant issues and to select those with influence.

San Francisco 1998

Rather than conducting individual meetings with city commissioners, the Commission on the Status of Women brought together women commissioners throughout San Francisco for a briefing on CEDAW. These commissioners then supported the resolution in their commissions.

In San Francisco, the San Francisco Board of Supervisors unanimously passed a resolution that supported the United States ratification of CEDAW and committed itself to the implementation of CEDAW within the City and County of San Francisco. This initial resolution was what enabled representatives from the task force to encourage the city to truly integrate the standards of CEDAW through a city ordinance.

Public Hearings

A public hearing for elected and appointed officials is one of several possible means of reaching large numbers of people and demonstrating broad community support.

Public Forums

- Public hearing: A city office or department provides an opportunity for members of the public to address them, testify, make specific recommendations, and ask for change.
- Briefing: A panel of experts presents recommendations on a specific issue to a city commission or department.
- Town hall meeting: Provides a place for people to gather, talk, and express opinions on a topic.

Questions to Ask as You Are Beginning to Plan a Public Forum

1. Who is your primary audience? Why?

2. Who is your secondary audience?

3. What do you want from your audiences?

4. What kind of support or decisions do you need?

5. Which public forum is most effective or familiar for your audience?

6. Where are you in your overall implementation timeline?

7. How much time do you have before you need to reach your audience?

What Are the Goals of a Public Hearing on CEDAW?

- Demonstrate the relevance of human rights and CEDAW to local communities.

- Increase awareness and document systemic discrimination faced by women and girls.

- Provide public education about women and human rights.

- Obtain commitments of support from officials.

- Create a forum for public officials to display their commitment to human rights.

Remember: a public hearing is not the end but only a forum that can be used as the means to change.

San Francisco 1998

The task force decided to coordinate a public hearing before the San Francisco Board of Supervisors as a means of educating policymakers and other decision-makers about the human rights of women and girls in San Francisco and hold them accountable to protecting these rights. In most US cities, a public hearing would be before the city council. Because San Francisco is both a city and county, the Board of Supervisors is our elected decision-making body. The hearings facilitated a public exchange of ideas and demands between community members, service providers, advocates, and city officials. It highlighted the relevance of CEDAW in people's lives and the systemic discrimination faced by women because of their gender. We asked the panelists to provide their reflections and thoughts on what they heard during the testimony. This led them to commit publicly to uphold the principles of CEDAW by implementing its standards through gender analysis and integration in employment, service delivery, and allocation of funds.

Many of the task force members had witnessed firsthand how women's groups from around the world use hearings and tribunals to ensure that their voices are heard by those who make the decisions that affect the lives of women and girls. We chose a public hearing because the city government is familiar with this form of community expression, and it enabled us to reach a broad constituency who either attended or watched the hearing on public access television.

When Should We Hold a Public Hearing?

- Determine how long key public officials and decision-makers will be in office. If possible, time your hearing so that most of your key supporters will be in office at least six months after the hearing date. (City commission members are usually appointed by the mayor.)

- Determine when you should not hold a hearing. For example, make sure the hearing is coordinated with budget cycles and election cycles. Never hold a public hearing right before elections or in the middle or end of a budget planning process.

- Make sure the hearing falls within a month of a key strategic moment related to your overall implementation timeline and keep in mind community activities and schedules. For example, choose strategic times with coordinated holidays and events, such as Black History Month in February, International Women's Day on March 8, Gay Pride in June, Domestic Violence Awareness Month and Indigenous People's Day in October, or Human Rights Day on December 10.

- A hearing can happen at different points, such as when you are ready to pass a resolution or after a resolution has been passed, and before a vote on an ordinance.

Who Should Attend a Public Hearing?

Overall, the answer to this question has to do with what you are looking for from your audience and key-decision makers.

1. Government: Who do you want to be there from government, based on what to accomplish (e.g., two-thirds of Board of Supervisors, the powerful city departments and those that impact the lives of women and the budget)? Who are the decision-makers? If you are sure your choice can't make it, do you want staff members to attend?

2. Experts/panelists: Who are the officials or members of the public you will select, who will listen to and comment on the testimony? Who will listen to what people have to say and to the recommendations the community is making?

3. Testifiers: Who are credible community members and advocates who can provide accurate, focused, and concise testimony?

4. The public: Whom do you want in the audience? What constituencies can you bring through working with your community supporters and doing media outreach?

5. Media leaders and influencers

6. Private sector organizations and leaders

Who Should We Invite to Be the Panelists at a Public Hearing?

Panelists can make commitments on behalf of their organizations or role in the community and will bring back information to the communities they work in. You may want to consider selecting:

1. Monetary decision-makers (e.g., elected officials, the chair of the budget committee)

2. People who can implement CEDAW (e.g., heads of city departments)

3. Allies

San Francisco 1998

In San Francisco, we asked all the members of the Board of Supervisors to attend the public hearing and to support and pass a resolution.

How Should We Select and Prepare Public Hearing Speakers?

1. Ask community leaders to speak who are working on specific issues that demonstrate the relevance of CEDAW. Some of them may have attended a CEDAW workshop and may be part of your task force. Also ask task force members to identify individuals and organizations that should participate. Include both advocates and service providers.

2. Call and ask them about their work, areas of expertise, and what issues are important to them.

3. Based on this conversation, send them a letter and information about which CEDAW article they will be addressing. Also include contact information for task force members; the more information you provide, the better.

4. Keep in close touch, especially right after they receive the letter and information and on the day before the hearing. If possible, meet with them in person. Inform them about what you want from the city officials. In some cases, you may want to run through their testimony with them and talk with them at length about how to link their testimony specifically to CEDAW.

5. Ask beforehand what recommendations people plan to make so that they are consistent with your goals; don't ever assume that you know their position.

San Francisco 1998

In San Francisco, the task force created subcommittees in three issue areas with local relevance: violence, health, and economic justice. Each of these committees was responsible for selecting five speakers from the community. They spent about two months researching their issue and recruiting speakers.

Although some of the people who were asked to speak at the public hearing had attended a CEDAW workshop, most were unfamiliar with CEDAW. To make sure that every speaker felt comfortable addressing their topic in relation to the relevant article of CEDAW, staff members at WILD for Human Rights spoke with them at length about women's human rights and CEDAW. Staff also sent them a form that verified the topic and CEDAW article they were asked to address as well as a copy of the full treaty with relevant articles highlighted.

At the hearing, many of the speakers specifically indicated somewhere in their statement that they were addressing a particular article from CEDAW, and most of them presented specific recommendations.

How Do We Get the Public and City Officials Involved in Public Hearings?

Encourage all community groups that signed up to support CEDAW to send people. Ask the testifiers to bring other people from their organizations. Invite community groups that you think will support CEDAW in the future. You may want to ask supporters to wear buttons or ribbons to show their support. You also should consider to what extent you want to control the hearing format, collect public questions, and leave time for open comments from the public.

Reach out to city officials to commit to CEDAW Pledges, publicize these and engage them from the beginning to help organize public hearings; livestream official hearings at city hall and record them on YouTube.

Check out the "Creating a Media Strategy" section for more information about reaching the public through local media sources.

San Francisco 1998

While the subcommittees were selecting speakers, the task force created a flyer that notified community members about the public hearing and asked them to attend as observers. Knowing that the size of the audience would give an impact on the panelists, we worked very hard to get a number of community members to attend the hearing. The key organizations affiliated with the task force sent a flyer to everyone on their mailing lists. The event also was advertised in the calendar of events of a Bay Area weekly newspaper.

We scripted the San Francisco public hearing very tightly and left little time at the end for public comments. In general, a format with preselected speakers worked well, allowing the hearings to move quickly. However, we also found that the community members who spoke at the end of the hearing ended up being some of the most memorable and dynamic speakers of the whole evening.

We would recommend leaving more time than we did, because public comments can provide additional real-life examples that educate and galvanize the panelists. However, keep in mind that the risk in doing so is that those with opposing views might also speak, especially in more conservative locales.

Public Hearing Pitfalls to Avoid:

- While looking for a diversity of people to testify, do not tokenize or stereotype. Instead, go beyond stereotypes by selecting speakers who challenge expectations. Make sure that men testify.

- Make the holistic nature of human rights visible by presenting a range of testimonies on several issue areas. CEDAW addresses multiple issue areas that represent the complex issues women face in our lives; do not push a single-issue agenda.

- Do not plan a hearing that is politically partisan because it will not further the rights of women and girls.

- Do not let speakers testify for longer than three minutes. A prepared statement will easily convey their needs and recommendations in three minutes. Look at their statements beforehand, if possible.

- Do not plan a hearing that is longer than two hours.

- Collect the statements in writing to distribute later to officials.

San Francisco 1998

One of the biggest challenges that we encountered while organizing the public hearing was the amount of logistical work needed to make the event successful. Although it worked very well to have specific task force members responsible for recruiting speakers for each issue area, most of the follow-up work and logistics were done by the staff at WILD for Human Rights. Likewise, the city Commission on the Status of Women was responsible for all the invitations to panelists and the follow up with individuals who agreed to be panelists. It may be important to recognize that certain logistics will have to be coordinated by one organization or person and to plan accordingly in advance.

Public Hearing Planning Tips:

- Select people, including men as well as women, who are diverse by age, race, gender, sexual orientation, class, and religion, to testify. Make sure the most vulnerable communities are addressed or represented at the hearing (e.g., homeless youth, incarcerated women, immigrant women).

- Select people to testify who are experienced and credible to both public officials and community members. Include at least one personal testimony for each of the issue areas that you cover, one well-known respected official (e.g., a judge), and a minimum of one male in each of the issue areas.

- Ask each speaker to relate their testimony explicitly to human rights and a specific CEDAW article.

- Put together a packet of information for legislators that includes a list of your supporters, background information, and a copy of CEDAW.

- Get commitments from city officials at the end of the hearing!

- At the beginning, middle, and end of the hearing, state your demands and recommendations. The opening and closing of the hearing can be five to seven minutes long.

San Francisco 1998

Since a public hearing is sponsored by a member of the Board of Supervisors and takes place in the chambers of the Board of Supervisors, it is bound by strict time limits. To maximize the impact of the hearing and to ensure that we were able to address the three issue areas, we had to set strict time limits for each of the speakers.

The public hearing opened with an eight-minute introduction to CEDAW presented by one of the co-chairs of the task force, who laid out the format of the hearing as well as the demands of the community. The community demands were: (1) implementation of CEDAW, (2) budget allocations for implementation, and (3) gender analysis of selected city departments' employment, budget, and service delivery. Following the presentation, the testifying speakers spoke for three minutes each in clusters of five according to the three issue areas: economic development, violence against women, and women's health. The public hearing concluded with an eight-minute statement made by another number of the task force from one of the partner organizations, who again presented the general recommendations and demands of the community. A strategy that we used to make the hearing as effective as possible was to begin each issue area with a powerful speaker. We also tried to create a balance in each issue area between those who were testifying based on their personal experiences, and those who were testifying based on their work or observations.

Remember: *The process is about building relationships and partnerships with people you respect.*

Attaining a City Ordinance

What Do We Need to Know First?

Passing an ordinance is not the only way to implement CEDAW. However, it makes it a law. A law will not change easily based on who is in charge. A law can include budgetary implications and commitments, and it will be enforceable and proactive rather than reactionary.

Before you enter the legislative process, you should make sure you understand how the process will unfold in your jurisdiction, whom your legislative contact is, and which of the affected governmental and non-governmental parties should be consulted. You must develop an advocacy strategy based on whose support you need to obtain.

If an ordinance seems like the best approach, find out how ordinances are passed in your city. If ordinances go through committee(s) as well as through a governing board or council, you will need to meet with committee members as well as with the entire board. When you conduct these meetings, you will need to state clearly why implementing CEDAW through an ordinance is important and demonstrate public support.

Always provide a "one-pager," a summary of information, or "talking points," a short list of key ideas for your allies.

The importance of doing your homework cannot be overstated. Although each city, county, state, or country has its own methods for drafting laws, some basic aspects probably remain the same:

- A legislative member must introduce the bill. This means that it is critical to receive the support of a legislator.

- The staff of this legislator probably will have to be involved in drafting the bill.

- Other interested parties who may support or oppose the bill must be able to review and comment on the bill, or else the bill may not get very far.

San Francisco 1998

In San Francisco, according to the City Attorney's office of San Francisco, the legislative process is as follows:

Generally, a member of the Board of Supervisors, the mayor, or a department head requests that the City Attorney's Office draft an ordinance. Once the ordinance is drafted by the City Attorney's Office, a member of the Board of Supervisors or the mayor submits the ordinance to the clerk, who forwards it to the board for introduction. (San Francisco Charter sec. 2.105.) The ordinance must then be referred to and reported upon by an appropriate committee of the board. (ibid.)

Once a committee hears and recommends approval of the ordinance, the ordinance is referred to the full board for consideration. The Board of Supervisors must vote to approve an ordinance at two separate meetings held at least five days apart. (San Francisco Charter sec. 2.105.) If the ordinance is amended at its second reading, the ordinance requires an additional reading not fewer than five days later prior to the final passage. (ibid.)

After the board has finally approved an ordinance, the ordinance is delivered to the mayor on the following day for consideration. The mayor has 10 days to determine whether to sign or disapprove the ordinance. (San Francisco Charter sec. 3.103.) If the mayor disapproves an ordinance, he returns it to the board of Supervisors. (ibid.) The board may then override the mayor's veto by a two-thirds vote. (San Francisco Charter sec. 2.106). If the mayor takes no action on the ordinance, it is deemed approved 10 days after the delivery of the ordinance to him. (San Francisco Charter sec. 3.103.)

Once the mayor has approved the ordinance (or it becomes effective without the mayor's signature), the ordinance takes effect no sooner than 30 days later. (San Francisco Charter sec. 2.105.)

How Can We Get Support for an Ordinance?

As stated above, it is critical to get local government support as soon as possible, and your contacts should be in place long before the public hearing. You should research all members of the legislative body: their politics, personalities, and relative power within the legislature.

It will not do you much good to work with a legislator who agrees with you if that individual does not have the political clout necessary to support your work. You can do research through talking to colleagues, following media coverage of local politics, and looking at voting records. Once you have located a few likely candidates, contact them with a detailed proposal setting forth what you want to do and why. Hopefully, your media campaign and workshop materials will have supplied you with lots of background information that you can give them to demonstrate the importance of your work. You should also meet with government departments that may be affected by the proposed ordinance. These officials are crucial to your success because they will invite you to participate in the process of drafting the ordinance.

Important: Before entering this process, you must research the state and federal laws on non-profit lobbying. Many countries, including the United States, limit the amount of direct action charitable 501 (c) (3) organizations can make towards drafting and passing legislation. If you do not want to jeopardize your non-profit status or the status of any of your partners, review your relevant regulations and make sure that you do not overstep these boundaries. If a government body gives you a written request for technical assistance on drafting legislation, you will not jeopardize your status by assisting them. In the US, you may want to consider working with an organization that has a 501 (c) (4) status or an organization permitted to lobby. Throughout the process, also make sure that your Board of Directors know what you are doing.

If you are a government body, your job in drafting and passing legislation is easier. But you must make extra efforts to partner with a reputable community-based organization and build a coalition to ensure you have community input. It will be very easy and tempting to draft the law without this input, but the resulting bill will not have the credibility, and consequently the impact, that you want.

In either case, when trying to garner support for the bill, you must emphasize how the bill will benefit the constituency of the group or official with whom you are talking.

Drafting Tips

- Take the time at the start of the process to dream about your vision for the ideal law and its implementation.

- Be clear about your bottom lines: what you are not willing to negotiate about or remove from the ordinance, including money and budget items.

- Respect the government drafters' concerns and experience. They may provide an important reality check, but they may be too cautious. It's a balancing act.

- Do not draft an ordinance that does not include budgetary support for enforcement.

- Develop an effective enforcement mechanism.

- Keep the focus on human rights.

- The more city departments and unions that know about the law and support its goals, the more effective it will be after its passage.

- Hold thematic town meetings with community groups on topics such as sex work, race, domestic violence, health, and sexual orientation issues. These meetings will allow you to get feedback during the drafting process about possible impacts on relevant communities.

- Keep in mind the populations who are most marginalized. Will this legislation have a positive impact on the quality of their lives? This will help ensure that you do not leave something out or argue for, and then include a provision that will end up harming the communities you want to assist and serve.

Case Study of San Francisco in 1998

In the case of the CEDAW ordinance in San Francisco in 1998, Board of Supervisor's President Barbara Kaufman held a public hearing on October 30, 1996. After the public hearing, the Board of Supervisors passed a resolution supporting the implementation of CEDAW in San Francisco. In addition, the CEDAW ordinance had the support of San Francisco's Commission on the Status of Women, which sponsored the bill.

Drafting the San Francisco CEDAW ordinance was a collaborative process which took several months because we did not have any prior models for local adoption of international treaties. At our first meeting we set our vision of what a women's human rights law should do and cover. We used information gathered from community task force meetings and testimony from the public hearings to develop recommendations on what women and girls in San Francisco need in order to have their human rights protected. We also described our ideal enforcement mechanism. Legal and political realities informed our discussions, but it was very useful to imagine our ideal law.

Based on our discussions, the city attorney produced a draft law. At each meeting, participants would provide comments on subsequent drafts of the law. WILD for Human Rights staff provided suggestions on the draft considering human rights law, our sense of what community groups needed and wanted, and how those interests could be met through human rights law. Although the task force advocated for as strong a law as possible, we also tried to be sensitive to the government drafters' concerns, and when they said that a certain provision was critical or conversely that a provision would kill the law, we respected their opinion. But if the task force felt a compromise would destroy the objective of the law, we would make certain that was clear.

In most cases, disputes led to in-depth discussions that gave all concerned a greater understanding of what would be needed to have a strong, enforceable women's human rights law in San Francisco. For example, a few of the provisions suggested were against Proposition 209, a California State Initiative that severely restricts affirmative action. Despite our view that Proposition 209 violates human rights standards, the task force understood the city government's unwillingness to provoke a lawsuit. Rather, the task force suggested emphasizing the role the ordinance would play in providing evidence of ongoing discrimination, which is required under Prop. 209 to maintain any affirmative action program.

We also worked to develop an effective enforcement mechanism. We wanted to make sure that the ordinance did not represent "paper rights" but rather rights that can be accessed and used. The task force wanted to connect the law to the budget process. However, several drafters thought this could jeopardize support for the bill. As a result, WILD for Human Rights suggested regular public meetings about CEDAW implementation, which would maintain accountability, and the future development of action plans that eventually could be tied to budgets. Ultimately, after the ordinance passed, the city budgeted $200,000 for the first years of implementation.

Once the bill was finalized, WILD for Human Rights continued to participate in the implementation process. We helped explain the law to relevant parts of the city government. We prepared documents that set forth the significance of this San Francisco ordinance, its national relevance, and its connection to CEDAW. In addition, we responded to all questions from government staff about the law and provided support when necessary. At the Board of Supervisors committee hearing, we spoke in support of the bill and emphasized its wider national and global significance.

The drafting process led to a strong city ordinance with two main parts. First, it established an official CEDAW Task Force, which consisted of four government and five community members, including those familiar with local issues and those familiar with women's human rights. (This Task Force is not the same as the community task force that the partner organizations coalesced to pass the ordinance.) The CEDAW Task Force reported to the Mayor, Board of Supervisors, and Commission on the Status of Women (COSW) every six months. Second, COSW conducted a gender analysis on selected city departments. The COSW hired consultants who developed gender guidelines in collaboration with the CEDAW Task Force.

These guidelines included an evaluation of gender equality in allocation of funding, employment practice, delivery of direct and indirect services, and operations. The analyses go beyond quantity to examine the quality of the funding, employment, and services. The guidelines emphasized that not only do health and human services departments impact women's human rights, but that all departments can impact women's rights.

After completing the gender analysis, COSW submitted action plans that addressed the deficiencies found via the gender studies of selected departments, described remedial actions to correct those deficiencies, and set forth the actions each department should take to implement CEDAW principles. In addition, COSW trained the selected departments in gender analysis and will continue to train all departments in human rights with a gender perspective.

Creating A Media Strategy

cities for cedaw

For Discussion

- Who can you identify to help you develop a media strategy?

- Do members of your coalition or partners have media focal points or expertise?

- How can you best use social media?

- Have you put enough safeguards and protections online for your media campaign?

- Have you assigned members of your coalition to track the opposition's media?

- How can you get media partners from the very beginning of your campaign?

Media is a vital tool for public education and influence. If you are asking people to change their way of viewing the world, they need information. Through media, a broad audience can become aware of discrimination within local communities and how discrimination violates international human rights and therefore, they begin to look for remedies beyond domestic policies and law.

In addition to increasing the visibility of discrimination against women and girls, you can promote the importance of implementing human rights standards within local

Beijing Platform for Action 1995

Women and media c. [Governments should] Encourage and recognize women's media networks, including electronic networks and other new technologies of communication as a means for the dissemination of information and the exchange of views, including at the international level, and support women's groups active in all media work and systems of communications to that end....

communities in the United States. This means working with both local reporters and international reporters. You will probably need to decide which group to target and then create a media strategy. In the best-case scenario, you will be able to work with both groups of journalists. In almost all cases, you will have to convince journalists of the importance of reporting about women's human rights.

Tips for Working With the Media

- Be responsive to journalists and make sure you are easily reachable.

- Start your media work immediately. This includes developing current contacts and finding funding specifically for media outreach.

- One committee of your task force should be dedicated solely to media, with clear responsibility for media outreach, drafting opinion and editorial pieces ("op-eds"), writing press releases and letters to the editor, pitching articles to journalists, and talking to media at events.

- Determine who covers your issue. Contact your community based web news, influences and podcast creators.

- Make sure that your coalition's name and phone number(s) are on all the materials that get distributed. This will ensure that you are contacted for comment.

- Monitor the opposition's statements on social media and other outlets.

- Draft press releases for relevant events that include what you are asking for and why you need it. Create headlines that will grab leaders' attention. Don't include unusual cases that have never happened before (i.e., if your city generally does a good job but didn't this time). Include quotations from the partner organizations and information about how the public can get involved.

- Develop sound bites to get your point across concisely and persuasively for television and radio in one to two sentences. Prepare "talking points," a short list of key ideas that you want to get across, for task force members so that their sound bites are accurate and informative. Designate one task force member from the media committee as your media spokesperson.

- Write and send articles to news sources to get their attention.

- If possible, ask key members of city government to co-host a press briefing with you to introduce a resolution or an ordinance.

- Journalists need stories. Develop a list of contact names and organizations familiar with human rights violations in your city that you can provide to journalists. With the permission of the people who are having their rights violated, put their stories in your op-eds and make their phone numbers and basic stories available when the press calls. If you publicize the stories behind the law, journalists will write about the law.

- Remember to cultivate press contacts and give them plenty of advance warning about actions and events. Try to view media work as a long-term education process, which may not result in immediate coverage but could do so in the future.

- Media work takes time, more than you would probably think. Therefore, it is important to start right away.

- Use the internet to check major media outlets and research relevant coverage in online magazines and other social sites. You can also post your news on related LISTSERVs.

San Francisco 1998

Our task force wanted to raise public awareness about human rights. We did not have enough money to have an extensive media plan, so we focused on getting press coverage for the public hearing and for the passage of the San Francisco CEDAW Ordinance. We believed these were the most newsworthy events. We also did national outreach on the ordinance passage to encourage more communities to consider implementing human rights. In the long term, we hoped to increase the media's interest in, and knowledge about, women's human rights in the United States. Our efforts were most successful when we had a strong press release and conducted comprehensive follow-up with journalists.

We decided to contact national and local journalists who have demonstrated interest in women's rights and thus use their knowledge to encourage them to think about human rights. One tactic that we did not use because of the lack of time and labor was to put up flyers or posters around the city announcing the public hearing and reaching out to a broad spectrum of community groups. As a result, most of the community members who attended the hearing were already involved with the task force, affiliated with one of the sponsoring organizations, or had attended one of our CEDAW workshops.

Since education and awareness were the primary goals of the CEDAW campaign, the task force arranged for both photographs and a tape recording of the hearing. Because the hearing took place in the Board of Supervisors's chambers, a public access cable channel in San Francisco recorded the hearing and broadcasted it numerous times. An unedited video recording of the hearing could also be easily purchased from the station.

From Local To Global

How Can I Connect to the Global Efforts for Women's Human Rights?

Connecting Local to Global is Critical

The Cities for CEDAW campaign can bring its innovation and leadership to the international arena.

↓

International feminist and women's movements can benefit from the experiences of the Cities for CEDAW campaign.

1. NGOCSW/NY award and trainings during CSW is a hub for this campaign (www.ngocsw.org)
2. The CEDAW Committee: https://www.ohchr.org/en/treaty-bodies/cedaw
3. UN Habitat (https://unhabitat.org) ICLEI (https://iclei.org) and Metropolis (https://www.metropolis.org) women's leadership
☐ The Global Compact partners to achieve UN goals (https://unglobalcompact.org)

Why should your campaign pay attention to connecting the local to the global? Connecting local work to global allows us to share our experiences with others as well as learn from promising practices in other parts of the world. The Cities for CEDAW campaign can bring its innovation and leadership to the international arena. This is useful to learn from other countries like Iceland,

Austria, and Colombia that have had longer experiences localizing human rights treaties.[7] At the same time, the Cities for CEDAW campaign can also contribute to the international effort for CEDAW implementation because many countries which have ratified the treaty have not implemented fully at the local level.

How can you connect back to the global level? You can make contacts locally that can be very valuable. Many of the local coalitions have ties to the UN through international NGOs like UNA/USA, Zonta, the League of Women Voters, or the International Alliance of Women. These NGOs often organize delegations to the annual UN Commission on the Status of Women which oversees the implementation of the Beijing Platform for Action. The CSW also has an NGO Forum convened by the NGOCSW/NY. In 2022, there were more than 35,000 virtual NGO participants, and in the future, the NGO Forum is likely to be hybrid, holding both virtual and in-person meetings. Attendance at the NGO Forum is free and open for registration every year in the fall. For information, see www.NGOCSW.org.

CEDAW General Recommendation 30 on Women in conflict prevention, conflict and post-conflict situations

Under the Convention, States parties' obligations to prevent, investigate and punish trafficking and sexual and gender-based violence are reinforced by international criminal law, including jurisprudence of the international and mixed criminal tribunals and the Rome State of the International Criminal Court, pursuant to which enslavement in the course of trafficking in women and girls, rape, sexual slavery, enforced prostitution, forced pregnancy, enforced sterilization or any other form of sexual violence of comparable gravity may constitute a war crime, a crime against humanity or an act of torture, or constitute an act of genocide.

---

7   See Innovations for Equity: Cities for CEDAW https://www.youtube.com/watch?v=rogbRjLDWSs&t=38s

The UN also has several events which are important for governments and civil society active in the Cities for CEDAW campaign. This includes:

1. The CEDAW Committee with 23 elected experts is the body within the Human Rights Council that reviews government reports on CEDAW implementation. NGOs can submit shadow reports commenting on the official reports if governments are reporting. Note that since the US has not ratified CEDAW, they cannot serve on the committee. Nor does it submit periodic reports. However, the Cities for CEDAW has submitted two reports during informal lunch sessions. These have led to constructive dialogues and CEDAW expert opinions have helped inform the campaign's direction. Most CEDAW sessions can be seen on UN TV and NGOs can attend in-person during open sessions. For more information on their sessions, see: https://www.ohchr.org/en/treaty-bodies/cedaw

2. The UN High Level Political Forum that reviews the Sustainable Development Goals, including Goal 5 on Gender Equality (https://hlpf.un.org/home). NGOs and city officials can join one of the nine major groups that include women, youth, NGOs, local authorities professionals, private sector, etc.

3. UN Women (https://www.unwomen.org/en) is the UN entity under the UN Economic and Social Commission that is responsible to set the normative standards and help governments implement shared goals. In particular, it supports CEDAW policies and frameworks and is a reliable source of global information and action through the Generation Equality Forum (https://forum.generationequality.org/events-consultations). Youth groups are a vital part of this Forum as in all UN Women programs.

4. UN Habitat (https://unhabitat.org) holds regional and global meetings bringing together mayors, governors, and other civil society stakeholders as well as business owners, architects, city planners, and NGOs. The World Urban Campaign is the NGO counterpart holding a Women's Assembly at most of its meetings, along with Youth Assemblies and other civil society groups. UN Habitat also works closely with city network like ICLEI (https://iclei.org) and Metropolis (https://www.metropolis.org) that have special programs on gender equality and women's empowerment, particularly women's leadership.

5. The Global Compact is open to all businesses and civil society leaders to address how the private sector can be effective partners to achieve UN goals (https://unglobalcompact.org), including the SDGs and gender equality. This UN body holds annual gatherings at the regional as well as global level and can be an important place to network with small and large businesses.

6. The experiences of US feminist and women's movements can make important contributions to the global effort to implement CEDAW because localization is needed everywhere. Villages, towns, as well as cities, counties, and states, can work together—bottom-up—to help ensure that the hopes and dreams of future generations can lead to a safer, more equitable, peaceful, and healthy planet.

APPENDIX I: CEDAW

Convention on the Elimination of All Forms of Discrimination against Women

Adopted and opened for signature, ratification and accession by General Assembly resolution 34/180 of 18 December 1979 entry into force 3 September 1981, in accordance with article 27(1) The States Parties to the present Convention,

Noting that the Charter of the United Nations reaffirms faith in fundamental human rights, in the dignity and worth of the human person and in the equal rights of men and women,

Noting that the Universal Declaration of Human Rights affirms the principle of the inadmissibility of discrimination and proclaims that all human beings are born free and equal in dignity and rights and that everyone is entitled to all the rights and freedoms set forth therein, without distinction of any kind, including distinction based on sex,

Noting that the States Parties to the International Covenants on Human Rights have the obligation to ensure the equal rights of men and women to enjoy all economic, social, cultural, civil and political rights,

Considering the international conventions concluded under the auspices of the United Nations and the specialized agencies promoting equality of rights of men and women,

Noting also the resolutions, declarations and recommendations adopted by the United Nations and the specialized agencies promoting equality of rights of men and women,

Concerned, however, that despite these various instruments extensive discrimination against women continues to exist,

Recalling that discrimination against women violates the principles of equality of rights and respect for human dignity, is an obstacle to the participation of women, on equal terms with men, in the political, social, economic and cultural life of their countries, hampers the growth of the prosperity of society and the family and makes more difficult the full development of the potentialities of women in the service of their countries and of humanity,

Concerned that in situations of poverty women have the least access to food, health, education, training and opportunities for employment and other needs,

Convinced that the establishment of the new international economic order based on equity and justice will contribute significantly towards the promotion of equality between men and women,

Emphasizing that the eradication of apartheid, all forms of racism, racial discrimination, colonialism, neo-colonialism, aggression, foreign occupation and domination and interference in the internal affairs of States is essential to the full enjoyment of the rights of men and women,

Affirming that the strengthening of international peace and security, the relaxation of international tension, mutual co-operation among all States irrespective of their social and economic systems, general and complete disarmament, in particular nuclear disarmament under strict and effective international control, the affirmation of the principles of justice, equality and mutual benefit in relations among countries and the realization of the right of peoples under alien and colonial domination and foreign occupation to self-determination and independence, as well as respect for national sovereignty and territorial integrity, will promote social progress and development and as a consequence will contribute to the attainment of full equality between men and women,

Convinced that the full and complete development of a country, the welfare of the world and the cause of peace require the maximum participation of women on equal terms with men in all fields,

Bearing in mind the great contribution of women to the welfare of the family and to the development of society, so far not fully recognized, the social significance of maternity and the role of both parents in the family and in the upbringing of children, and aware that the role of women in procreation should not be a basis for discrimination but that the upbringing of children requires a sharing of responsibility between men and women and society as a whole,

Aware that a change in the traditional role of men as well as the role of women in society and in the family is needed to achieve full equality between men and women,

Determined to implement the principles set forth in the Declaration on the Elimination of Discrimination against Women and, for that purpose, to adopt the measures required for the elimination of such discrimination in all its forms and manifestations,

Have agreed on the following:

PART I

Article 1

For the purposes of the present Convention, the term "discrimination against women" shall mean any distinction, exclusion or restriction made on the basis of sex which has the effect or purpose of impairing or nullifying the recognition, enjoyment or exercise by women, irrespective of their marital status, on a basis of equality of men and women, of human rights and fundamental freedoms in the political, economic, social, cultural, civil or any other field.

Article 2

States Parties condemn discrimination against women in all its forms, agree to pursue by all appropriate means and without delay a policy of eliminating discrimination against women and, to this end, undertake:

(a) To embody the principle of the equality of men and women in their national constitutions or other appropriate legislation if not yet incorporated therein and to ensure, through law and other appropriate means, the practical realization of this principle;

(b) To adopt appropriate legislative and other measures, including sanctions where appropriate, prohibiting all discrimination against women;

(c) To establish legal protection of the rights of women on an equal basis with men and to ensure through competent national tribunals and other public institutions the effective protection of women against any act of discrimination;

(d) To refrain from engaging in any act or practice of discrimination against women and to ensure that public authorities and institutions shall act in conformity with this obligation;

(e) To take all appropriate measures to eliminate discrimination against women by any person, organization or enterprise;

(f) To take all appropriate measures, including legislation, to modify or abolish existing laws, regulations, customs and practices which constitute discrimination against women;

(g) To repeal all national penal provisions which constitute discrimination against women.

Article 3

States Parties shall take in all fields, in particular in the political, social, economic and cultural fields, all appropriate measures, including legislation, to ensure the full development and advancement of women, for the purpose of guaranteeing them the exercise and enjoyment of human rights and fundamental freedoms on a basis of equality with men.

Article 4

1. Adoption by States Parties of temporary special measures aimed at accelerating de facto equality between men and women shall not be considered discrimination as defined in the present Convention, but shall in no way entail as a consequence the maintenance of unequal or separate standards; these measures shall be discontinued when the objectives of equality of opportunity and treatment have been achieved.

2. Adoption by States Parties of special measures, including those measures contained in the present Convention, aimed at protecting maternity shall not be considered discriminatory.

Article 5

States Parties shall take all appropriate measures:

(a) To modify the social and cultural patterns of conduct of men and women, with a view to achieving the elimination of prejudices and customary and all other practices which are based on the idea of the inferiority or the superiority of either of the sexes or on stereotyped roles for men and women;

(b) To ensure that family education includes a proper understanding of maternity as a social function and the recognition of the common responsibility of men and women in the upbringing and development of their children, it being understood that the interest of the children is the primordial consideration in all cases.

Article 6

States Parties shall take all appropriate measures, including legislation, to suppress all forms of traffic in women and exploitation of prostitution of women.

PART II

Article 7

States Parties shall take all appropriate measures to eliminate discrimination against women in the political and public life of the country and, in particular, shall ensure to women, on equal terms with men, the right:

(a) To vote in all elections and public referenda and to be eligible for election to all publicly elected bodies;

(b) To participate in the formulation of government policy and the implementation thereof and to hold public office and perform all public functions at all levels of government;

(c) To participate in non-governmental organizations and associations concerned with the public and political life of the country.

Article 8

States Parties shall take all appropriate measures to ensure to women, on equal terms with men and without any discrimination, the opportunity to represent their Governments at the international level and to participate in the work of international organizations.

Article 9

1. States Parties shall grant women equal rights with men to acquire, change or retain their nationality. They shall ensure in particular that neither marriage to an alien nor change of nationality by the husband during marriage shall automatically change the nationality of the wife, render her stateless or force upon her the nationality of the husband.

2. States Parties shall grant women equal rights with men with respect to the nationality of their children.

PART III

Article 10

States Parties shall take all appropriate measures to eliminate discrimination against women in order to ensure to them equal rights with men in the field of education and in particular to ensure, on a basis of equality of men and women:

(a) The same conditions for career and vocational guidance, for access to studies and for the achievement of diplomas in educational establishments of all categories in rural as well as in urban areas; this equality shall be ensured in pre-school, general, technical, professional and higher technical education, as well as in all types of vocational training;

(b) Access to the same curricula, the same examinations, teaching staff with qualifications of the same standard and school premises and equipment of the same quality;

(c) The elimination of any stereotyped concept of the roles of men and women at all levels and in all forms of education by encouraging coeducation and other types of education which will help to achieve this aim and, in particular, by the revision of textbooks and school programmes and the adaptation of teaching methods;

(d) The same opportunities to benefit from scholarships and other study grants;

(e) The same opportunities for access to programmes of continuing education, including adult and

functional literacy programmes, particularly those aimed at reducing, at the earliest possible time, any gap in education existing between men and women;

(f) The reduction of female student drop-out rates and the organization of programmes for girls and women who have left school prematurely;

(g) The same Opportunities to participate actively in sports and physical education;

(h) Access to specific educational information to help to ensure the health and well-being of families, including information and advice on family planning.

Article 11

1. States Parties shall take all appropriate measures to eliminate discrimination against women in the field of employment in order to ensure, on a basis of equality of men and women, the same rights, in particular:

(a) The right to work as an inalienable right of all human beings;

(b) The right to the same employment opportunities, including the application of the same criteria for selection in matters of employment;

(c) The right to free choice of profession and employment, the right to promotion, job security and all benefits and conditions of service and the right to receive vocational training and retraining, including apprenticeships, advanced vocational training and recurrent training;

(d) The right to equal remuneration, including benefits, and to equal treatment in respect of work of equal value, as well as equality of treatment in the evaluation of the quality of work;

(e) The right to social security, particularly in cases of retirement, unemployment, sickness, invalidity and old age and other incapacity to work, as well as the right to paid leave;

(f) The right to protection of health and to safety in working conditions, including the safeguarding of the function of reproduction.

2. In order to prevent discrimination against women on the grounds of marriage or maternity and to ensure their effective right to work, States Parties shall take appropriate measures:

(a) To prohibit, subject to the imposition of sanctions, dismissal on the grounds of pregnancy or of maternity leave and discrimination in dismissals on the basis of marital status;

(b) To introduce maternity leave with pay or with comparable social benefits without loss of former employment, seniority or social allowances;

(c) To encourage the provision of the necessary supporting social services to enable parents to combine family obligations with work responsibilities and participation in public life, in particular through promoting the establishment and development of a network of child-care facilities;

(d) To provide special protection to women during pregnancy in types of work proved to be harmful to them.

3. Protective legislation relating to matters covered in this article shall be reviewed periodically in the light of scientific and technological knowledge and shall be revised, repealed or extended as necessary.

Article 12

1. States Parties shall take all appropriate measures to eliminate discrimination against women in the field of health care in order to ensure, on a basis of equality of men and women, access to health care services, including those related to family planning.

2. Notwithstanding the provisions of paragraph I of this article, States Parties shall ensure to women appropriate services in connection with pregnancy, confinement and the post-natal period, granting free services where necessary, as well as adequate nutrition during pregnancy and lactation.

Article 13

States Parties shall take all appropriate measures to eliminate discrimination against women in other areas of economic and social life in order to ensure, on a basis of equality of men and women, the same rights, in particular:

(a) The right to family benefits;

(b) The right to bank loans, mortgages and other forms of financial credit;

(c) The right to participate in recreational activities, sports and all aspects of cultural life.

Article 14

1. States Parties shall take into account the particular problems faced by rural women and the significant roles which rural women play in the economic survival of their families, including their work in the non-monetized sectors of the economy, and shall take all appropriate measures to ensure the application of the provisions of the present Convention to women in rural areas.

2. States Parties shall take all appropriate measures to eliminate discrimination against women in rural areas in order to ensure, on a basis of equality of men and women, that they participate in and benefit from rural development and, in particular, shall ensure to such women the right:

(a) To participate in the elaboration and implementation of development planning at all levels;

(b) To have access to adequate health care facilities, including information, counselling and services in family planning;

(c) To benefit directly from social security programmes;

(d) To obtain all types of training and education, formal and non-formal, including that relating to functional literacy, as well as, inter alia, the benefit of all community and extension services, in order to increase their technical proficiency;

(e) To organize self-help groups and co-operatives in order to obtain equal access to economic opportunities through employment or self employment;

(f) To participate in all community activities;

(g) To have access to agricultural credit and loans, marketing facilities, appropriate technology and equal treatment in land and agrarian reform as well as in land resettlement schemes;

(h) To enjoy adequate living conditions, particularly in relation to housing, sanitation, electricity and water supply, transport and communications.

PART IV

Article 15

1. States Parties shall accord to women equality with men before the law.

2. States Parties shall accord to women, in civil matters, a legal capacity identical to that of men and the same opportunities to exercise that capacity. In particular, they shall give women equal rights to conclude contracts and to administer property and shall treat them equally in all stages of procedure in courts and tribunals.

3. States Parties agree that all contracts and all other private instruments of any kind with a legal effect which is directed at restricting the legal capacity of women shall be deemed null and void.

4. States Parties shall accord to men and women the same rights with regard to the law relating to the movement of persons and the freedom to choose their residence and domicile.

Article 16

1. States Parties shall take all appropriate measures to eliminate discrimination against women in all matters relating to marriage and family relations and in particular shall ensure, on a basis of equality of men and women:

(a) The same right to enter into marriage;

(b) The same right freely to choose a spouse and to enter into marriage only with their free and full consent;

(c) The same rights and responsibilities during marriage and at its dissolution;

(d) The same rights and responsibilities as parents, irrespective of their marital status, in matters relating to their children; in all cases the interests of the children shall be paramount;

(e) The same rights to decide freely and responsibly on the number and spacing of their children and to have access to the information, education and means to enable them to exercise these rights;

(f) The same rights and responsibilities with regard to guardianship, wardship, trusteeship and adoption of children, or similar institutions where these concepts exist in national legislation; in all cases the interests of the children shall be paramount;

(g) The same personal rights as husband and wife, including the right to choose a family name, a profession and an occupation;

(h) The same rights for both spouses in respect of the ownership, acquisition, management, administration, enjoyment and disposition of property, whether free of charge or for a valuable consideration.

2. The betrothal and the marriage of a child shall have no legal effect, and all necessary action, including legislation, shall be taken to specify a minimum age for marriage and to make the registration of marriages in an official registry compulsory.

PART V

Article 17

1. For the purpose of considering the progress made in the implementation of the present Convention, there shall be established a Committee on the Elimination of Discrimination against Women (hereinafter referred to as the Committee) consisting, at the time of entry into force of the Convention, of eighteen and, after ratification of or accession to the Convention by the thirty-fifth State Party of twenty-three experts of high moral standing and competence in the field covered by the Convention. The experts shall be elected by States Parties from among their nationals and shall serve in their personal capacity, consideration being given to equitable geographical distribution and to the representation of the different forms of civilization as well as the principal legal systems.

2. The members of the Committee shall be elected by secret ballot from a list of persons nominated by States Parties. Each State Party may nominate one person from among its own nationals.

3. The initial election shall be held six months after the date of the entry into force of the present Convention. At least three months before the date of each election the Secretary-General of the United Nations shall address a letter to the States Parties inviting them to submit their nominations within two months. The Secretary-General shall prepare a list in alphabetical order of all persons thus nominated, indicating the States Parties which have nominated them and shall submit it to the States Parties.

4. Elections of the members of the Committee shall be held at a meeting of States Parties convened by the Secretary-General at United Nations Headquarters. At that meeting, for which two thirds of the States Parties shall constitute a quorum, the persons elected to the Committee shall be those nominees who obtain the largest number of votes and an absolute majority of the votes of the representatives of States Parties present and voting.

5. The members of the Committee shall be elected for a term of four years. However, the terms of nine of the members elected at the first election shall expire at the end of two years; immediately after the first election the names of these nine members shall be chosen by lot by the Chairman of the Committee.

6. The election of the five additional members of the Committee shall be held in accordance with the provisions of paragraphs 2, 3 and 4 of this article, following the thirty-fifth ratification or accession.

The terms of two of the additional members elected on this occasion shall expire at the end of two years, the names of these two members having been chosen by lot by the Chairman of the Committee.

7. For the filling of casual vacancies, the State Party whose expert has ceased to function as a member of the Committee shall appoint another expert from among its nationals, subject to the approval of the Committee.

8. The members of the Committee shall, with the approval of the General Assembly, receive emoluments from United Nations resources on such terms and conditions as the Assembly may decide, having regard to the importance of the Committee's responsibilities.

9. The Secretary-General of the United Nations shall provide the necessary staff and facilities for the effective performance of the functions of the Committee under the present Convention.

Article 18

1. States Parties undertake to submit to the Secretary-General of the United Nations, for consideration by the Committee, a report on the legislative, judicial, administrative or other measures which they have adopted to give effect to the provisions of the present Convention and on the progress made in this respect:

(a) Within one year after the entry into force for the State concerned;

(b) Thereafter at least every four years and further whenever the Committee so requests.

2. Reports may indicate factors and difficulties affecting the degree of fulfilment of obligations under the present Convention.

Article 19

1. The Committee shall adopt its own rules of procedure.

2. The Committee shall elect its officers for a term of two years.

Article 20

1. The Committee shall normally meet for a period of not more than two weeks annually in order to consider the reports submitted in accordance with article 18 of the present Convention.

2. The meetings of the Committee shall normally be held at United Nations Headquarters or at any other convenient place as determined by the Committee.

Article 21

1. The Committee shall, through the Economic and Social Council, report annually to the General Assembly of the United Nations on its activities and may make suggestions and general recommendations based on the examination of reports and information received from the States Parties. Such suggestions and general recommendations shall be included in the report of the Committee together with comments, if any, from States Parties.

2. The Secretary-General of the United Nations shall transmit the reports of the Committee to the Commission on the Status of Women for its information.

Article 22

The specialized agencies shall be entitled to be represented at the consideration of the implementation of such provisions of the present Convention as fall within the scope of their activities. The Committee may invite the specialized agencies to submit reports on the implementation of the Convention in areas falling within the scope of their activities.

PART VI

Article 23

Nothing in the present Convention shall affect any provisions that are more conducive to the achievement of equality between men and women which may be contained:

(a) In the legislation of a State Party; or

(b) In any other international convention, treaty or agreement in force for that State.

Article 24

States Parties undertake to adopt all necessary measures at the national level aimed at achieving the full realization of the rights recognized in the present Convention.

Article 25

1. The present Convention shall be open for signature by all States.

2. The Secretary-General of the United Nations is designated as the depositary of the present Convention.

3. The present Convention is subject to ratification. Instruments of ratification shall be deposited with the Secretary-General of the United Nations.

4. The present Convention shall be open to accession by all States. Accession shall be effected by the deposit of an instrument of accession with the Secretary-General of the United Nations.

Article 26

1. A request for the revision of the present Convention may be made at any time by any State Party by means of a notification in writing addressed to the Secretary-General of the United Nations.

2. The General Assembly of the United Nations shall decide upon the steps, if any, to be taken in respect of such a request.

Article 27

1. The present Convention shall enter into force on the thirtieth day after the date of deposit with the Secretary-General of the United Nations of the twentieth instrument of ratification or accession.

2. For each State ratifying the present Convention or acceding to it after the deposit of the twentieth instrument of ratification or accession, the Convention shall enter into force on the thirtieth day after the date of the deposit of its own instrument of ratification or accession.

Article 28

1. The Secretary-General of the United Nations shall receive and circulate to all States the text of reservations made by States at the time of ratification or accession.

2. A reservation incompatible with the object and purpose of the present Convention shall not be permitted.

3. Reservations may be withdrawn at any time by notification to this effect addressed to the Secretary-General of the United Nations, who shall then inform all States thereof. Such notification shall take effect on the date on which it is received.

Article 29

1. Any dispute between two or more States Parties concerning the interpretation or application of the present Convention which is not settled by negotiation shall, at the request of one of them, be submitted to arbitration. If within six months from the date of the request for arbitration the parties are unable to agree on the organization of the arbitration, any one of those parties may refer the dispute to the International Court of Justice by request in conformity with the Statute of the Court.

2. Each State Party may at the time of signature or ratification of the present Convention or accession thereto declare that it does not consider itself bound by paragraph I of this article. The other States Parties shall not be bound by that paragraph with respect to any State Party which has made such a reservation.

3. Any State Party which has made a reservation in accordance with paragraph 2 of this article may at any time withdraw that reservation by notification to the Secretary-General of the United Nations.

Article 30

The present Convention, the Arabic, Chinese, English, French, Russian and Spanish texts of which are equally authentic, shall be deposited with the Secretary-General of the United Nations. IN WITNESS WHEREOF the undersigned, duly authorized, have signed the present Convention.

Krishanti Dharmaraj is a human rights advocate and a practitioner with three decades of experience working at the intersection of gender, race, and other identities at local, national, and global levels. She is the founder of Dignity Index, a methodology and a process to prevent and remedy structural discrimination and Dignidad360, an innovation lab to increase safety for women and girls in both public and private spheres. Krishanti is faculty at Glasgow Caledonian New York College, master's program in DEI Leadership. Krishanti was the executive director of center for Women's Global Leadership at Rutgers University, she initiated the US Human Rights Network and was the founding executive director of Women's Institute for Leadership Development (WILD) for Human Rights, where she spearheaded the work in San Francisco to pass legislation to implement an international human rights treaty-CEDAW.

Soon-Young Yoon is the UN representative for the International Alliance of Women. In 2021, she was appointed to the Council on Gender Equality convened by H. E. Ambassador, Abdhulla Shahid, the President of the 76th UN General Assembly. During her past tenure as chair of the NGO CSW/NY, the committee launched the Cities for CEDAW campaign in the US. In 2020, she founded and is currently co-director of the Cities for CEDAW History and Futures Project. She was a Social Development officer for UNICEF in the Southeast Asia office as well as the Social Scientist at WHO/SEARO in New Delhi. She serves as a board member of the International Foundation for Ewha Womans University and on the Global Advisory Board of the Harvard AIDS Initiative. A former columnist for the EarthTimes newspaper, she is co-editor with Dr Jonathan Samet of the WHO monograph, "Gender, Women, and the Tobacco Epidemic."

www.ingramcontent.com/pod-product-compliance
Lightning Source LLC
Chambersburg PA
CBHW042347030426
42335CB00031B/3483

* 9 7 8 1 9 6 1 3 0 2 3 7 2 *